"*Bridge the Gap* is ripe for the marketplace. It's a great resource for engaging resistant employees in diversity, inclusion, equity, and belonging work."

—MARILYN TAM
CEO of Marilyn Tam & Co. and founder and
Executive Director of Us Foundation, former CEO
of Aveda Corp., President of Reebok Apparel
and Retail Group, and VP of Nike Inc.

"In a sea of people talking over, at, or down to each other, *Bridge the Gap*, is that rare oasis that talks with you and teaches you to do the same so that you can pull people together in such a divided and divisive world."

—MARK GOULSTON, MD
author of *Just Listen*

"A compelling read that helps you see curiosity and communication through a new lens."

—ADAM MARKEL
author of *Change Proof*

"When business teams include participants from different political parties and perspectives everyone wins. This book will enhance the creation of diversity and help readers create bridges for individual and corporate success."

—JON FISHER
author of *I Took the Only Path to See You*
and founder of ViciNFT

"An innovative book for any professional! McCleary and Edwards embed their discussion of leadership at the intersection of your biology and lived experiences, recognizing the ways in which our approach to any situation in any given moment reflects the brain's state. The authors tap into modern conceptions of the brain from the field of neuroscience with colorful case studies rooted in real human dynamics."

—**LEONARD ABBEDUTO, PhD**
director UC Davis Mind Institute, professor,
Department of Psychiatry and Behavioral Sciences

"Cancel culture, polarization, and toxic language are harming our relationships—we can do better, and *Bridge the Gap* teaches you how."

—**SALLY EDWARDS**
founder and CEO, Heart Zones Inc.; cofounder, Fleet Feet;
cofounder, Yuba Snowshoe Company; cofounder,
Upbeat Workouts iPhone Mobile Apps

BRIDGE
THE
GAP

Breakthrough Communication Tools
to Transform Work Relationships From
Challenging to Collaborative

JENNIFER EDWARDS
AND KATIE McCLEARY

New York Chicago San Francisco Athens London Madrid
Mexico City Milan New Delhi Singapore Sydney Toronto

1 2 3 4 5 6 7 8 9   LCR   27 26 25 24 23 22

ISBN   978-1-264-26911-2
MHID   1-264-26911-0

e-ISBN   978-1-264-26912-9
e-MHID   1-264-26912-9

Library of Congress Cataloging-in-Publication Data

Names: Edwards, Jennifer (Business advisor), author. | McCleary, Katie, author.
Title: Bridge the gap : breakthrough communication tools to transform work relationships from challenging to collaborative / Jennifer Edwards and Katie McCleary.
Description: New York : McGraw Hill, [2022] | Includes bibliographical references and index.
Identifiers: LCCN 2021049780 (print) | LCCN 2021049781 (ebook) | ISBN 9781264269112 (hardback) | ISBN 9781264269129 (ebook)
Subjects: LCSH: Communication in management. | Communication in organizations. | Interpersonal communication. | Organizational behavior.
Classification: LCC HD30.3 .E296 2022 (print) | LCC HD30.3 (ebook) | DDC 658.4/5—dc23/eng/20211116
LC record available at https://lccn.loc.gov/2021049780
LC ebook record available at https://lccn.loc.gov/2021049781

McGraw Hill books are available at special quantity discounts to use as premiums and sales promotions or for use in corporate training programs. To contact a representative, please visit the Contact Us pages at www.mhprofessional.com.

McGraw Hill is committed to making our products accessible to all learners. To learn more about the available support and accommodations we offer, please contact us at accessibility@mheducation.com. We also participate in the Access Text Network (www.accesstext.org), and ATN members may submit requests through ATN.

CONTENTS

WHAT IT MEANS TO BRIDGE THE GAP

L et's just say it flat out.

You work with people that you struggle to understand, like, or respect. You also work with people who struggle to understand, like, or respect you.

As much as we would like our work relationships to be simple, unemotional, and confined to the 9-to-5 . . . the fact is that connecting, communicating, and collaborating with people is much more complex, time-consuming, and challenging.

Think back to the past month.

Has anyone at work pushed you over the edge with how confusing, irritating, or inept they are?

Have you sat in a team meeting and been annoyed about how your colleague is working through a problem because it's opposite of how you'd solve the situation?

Have you been offended by someone who made an aggressive comment during a work call, and it hijacked you away from the important task at hand?

Have you made an assumption about someone that was wrong, and it caused relational damage? Or conversely, when was the last time someone labeled, misjudged, and/or assumed something wrong about you and it impacted your work performance?

And last—probably the most common of all—what about a person at work who you simply don't understand? You can't figure out why they behave a certain way or say certain things. You struggle to relate to them at all: their personality, their hobbies or interests, their background or beliefs—and it's mucking up how you work with them because you can't connect to them and therefore this lack of connection is potentially damaging a relationship that you likely need to do your job well.

These situations happen all the time. And when they do—you face a moment of truth. You have a choice about how you respond and communicate.

You have a choice to step up and be the one that bridges the gap.

The depth and quality of your relationships matter, especially in the workplace. Rarely can you do it all alone—pioneer a new idea, create that product, manage a successful practice, write policy, hit the key performance indicators, fix the copy machine, post the social media, file taxes, manage the pipeline, fundraise the dollars—you need diversity of talent, skill, knowledge, and perspectives. It's highly likely that you need people who are different from you to help you accomplish your work and goals.

And frankly, our experiences of working with clients for forty combined years show one unifying theme: the most successful people in their careers are great communicators who are able to bridge the gap with people they struggle to:

1. Understand
2. Like
3. Respect

At work, you often don't get to choose your boss, colleagues, or clients, nor do you get the luxury of cherry-picking your professional relationships based on your particular preferences or needs. In fact, it's likely that you spend large parts of your workday with people who do not share your background, values, way of doing things, and/or perspective.

And what about those people who frustrate you to your breaking point: How do you communicate through those relationships?

Ignore them? Bad-mouth or gossip about them to your work buddies? Find every which way to avoid having to interact and speak with them?

Those strategies are train wrecks. The more you distance yourself from them, the larger the gap grows between you, and your quality of work suffers.

Anne had this exact same problem when we met her—she was at her wit's end with an esteemed colleague who annoyed her at every turn. She felt stuck in a professional relationship that was causing her to feel constant irritation, which sometimes made her snap. She was losing sleep and beginning to detest being the VP of Marketing of a major pharmaceutical company. All those years of ladder-climbing toward this dream job and finally earning it (and her amazing salary) was in jeopardy because of "that stupid Malcolm."

Dr. Malcolm, the head chemical engineer, is anything but stupid despite what Anne believes. For nearly a decade, he and his large team has been developing a revolutionary and life-saving heart medication that *finally* passed years of clinical trials and is ready to go to market. Anne's job is to design and lead a three-pronged national campaign with her small staff to market the drug to doctors, patients, and everyday people experiencing symptoms. In addition, her department must collaborate with sales to coalesce the campaign, branding, metrics, strategies, and outcomes. Anne is often stuck communicating between scientists, sales, creative, and her boss.

Of course, Anne loves (and needs) her job . . . but Dr. Malcolm is always there, Monday through Friday, getting under her skin with his constant negativity and naysaying about her team's ideas. In addition, Anne thinks he is unable to speak like a normal human being. He is constantly using scientific data and terms that most people don't understand—and he often digresses down rabbit holes and eventually mumbles things that Anne can't tell if they are important or not. To make matters worse, one time, Dr. Malcolm casually mentioned to their boss that he doesn't understand why Anne is always snippy and impatient with him. The boss shared this with Anne and basically told her to be nicer to Dr. Malcolm because "he is an important scientist who 'makes the magic happen.'" Anne is completely insulted by this because, from her perspective, everyone in the company makes the magic happen—not just Dr. Malcolm.

The relationship and communication gap between Anne and Dr. Malcolm is causing the launch to flatten and projected sales look grim. If Anne can't find a way to communicate better with Dr. Malcolm, she knows that her department will be thrown under the bus and likely blamed by the sales team for a poor launch. Eventually, she believes her boss will say "But Anne, I told you to work with Dr. Malcolm—he had all the answers about why people should buy the drug and ask their doctor for a prescription."

What is Anne to do? Can she bridge this critical gap?

Anne feels stuck in this situation. She is becoming hopeless. However, we reminded Anne that she is not powerless and has some choices to make about her options, which are:

- She can look for a new job if she simply can't face the pressure and stress anymore.
- She can stay and do nothing and continue to suffer.
- She can wish all day and night that Malcolm retires or that the boss will resolve the situation.
- She can continue to stress out that the launch and revenue will be negatively affected, and she'll continue losing sleep.
- Or she can choose to do something about the dynamics of this relationship that seems to be in perpetual breakdown. She can realize that Dr. Malcolm's behavior, or the situation, won't magically change (or at least in the timeframe she needs it to for the launch). She can choose to take to take personal responsibility and show up differently with new tactics because her success depends upon it.

Which choice do you think Anne should make? Ding! Ding! Ding!—it's the last one.

The same goes for you at work. Minute by minute, hour by hour, you have many opportunities to make a different choice about how you show up and bridge a gap in your relationships using clear and structured communication. Unfortunately, it can be dicey to get started because there are many internal and external factors at play that we are often unaware of. It is a little bit like the iceberg analogy. What you see above the water is only a fragment of what is below the water. There are large unseen iceberg-like factors—invisible forces—at play when you try to bridge the gap with the variety of people you work with daily. In this book, we will explore the internal and biological factors that impact human behavior, decision-making, and communication. We will give you tools, metaphors, and strategies to use to show up differently and communicate with more clarity when bridging the gap seems almost impossible.

However, we would be remiss if we didn't first acknowledge some significant external forces at play that are impacting your efforts.

LARGER EXTERNAL FORCES THAT WE'RE UP AGAINST

Navigating professional relationships these days is becoming increasingly bumpy.

- *Four generations of people wake up every day to go to work, together.* Boomers, Gen X, Millennials, and Gen Z are converging in one shared workplace.[1] In real time, we're contending with different generational and philosophical forms of management and leadership. We each seem to have different solutions and reactions to similar challenges. We are often attempting to achieve a similar ambition or goal but have wildly different communication styles and approaches. We're addressing gaps between skill, experience, and knowledge at any given moment. Essentially, we are not on the same page while attempting to achieve a shared outcome.
- *The personal and the professional are intermingling in new and surprising ways.* The rise of social media had already given us a glimpse into people's personal lives. Throw in a global pandemic, which created a warp-speed shift of "work-at-home" that many of us had never experienced, and we're seeing more of people's lives than we could have ever imagined. In particular, video-conferencing platforms

invite us into people's bedrooms and kitchens. We're witnessing how neat or sloppy they keep their personal space. We hear their kids, dogs, and toilets flushing in the background. We may see something personal that triggers us to question whether or not we can understand, like, or respect their character. In this landscape, the lines between the professional and personal are blurring, which can make communication even more tricky or awkward, especially if you're having to deliver feedback, present a professional presentation, or go through a formal evaluation.

- **We are working under the conditions of an increasingly polarized landscape of politics, race, and media disinformation.** Today, we are contending with "cancel culture,"[2] which makes so many people afraid to speak or ask questions for fear of misspeaking and offending someone. Cancel culture threatens to immediately discard and dismiss anyone who expresses a difference of opinion, even if that opinion is underdeveloped or expressed incorrectly. It's become extremely easy to dismiss, cancel, and/or criticize others who we believe are against us, not like us, or too different to understand.

- **Last, we're blind to the fact that each of us are part of the problem.** Sometimes we fail to see how our own preferences and perspectives, lived experiences, and personal agendas affect how we communicate with others. Communication starts long before words leave our mouths. It's well known that, more often than not, it's not *what you say* in a conversation that matters[3] as much as *how you show up* in the conversation. We simply are unaware of how we show up and the energy that we radiate to others.

Hands down, everyone (both at work and even at home and in our communities) needs updated skills to better navigate our relationships in this environment. Communicating with people in a fast-paced and stressful world is challenging and complex.

You're not alone though.

Most of us didn't consciously acquire communication and conversational skills—or sharpen them with repetitive practice on a consistent basis. In addition, very few of us ever learned how to be present with another person, to ignore internal and external noise and distractions, and to connect and converse with others in useful or collaborative ways.

It is for this reason that we have written this book and invite you to explore the information and tools with fresh curiosity. Every interaction you have has the power to improve or deteriorate a critical professional relationship. You have the power to propel the work forward by showing up with an intention to connect, engage, and communicate—even through tension, conflict, or awkwardness. Equally, you also have the power to shut people down, build divisive walls, create drama, shame and blame, and stonewall your own success and the company's progress.

Most of the time the choice is truly yours.

Of course, there are times when you may not have a choice—the other person might be sabotaging you, harassing you inappropriately, or thrashing your values because they are mean spirited. We call these canyons, not gaps, and we'll address those, too. However, overwhelmingly, most people are able to bridge gaps and enhance their work (and life) experience using our tools.

You *can* improve your relationships and communication, fundamentally shifting workplace dynamics for the better. And who knows? If you implement the tools (like Anne eventually did), you may even like your job more. You might even make some new friends. You might get tapped for a promotion or a raise because you're so good at bridging the gaps. If anything, you'll sleep better knowing you did your best, ready to wake up for another day at the office.

WHAT'S INSIDE THIS BOOK

We believe that how you show up—from your energy and presence to your listening and language—shapes most interactions and outcomes. In addition, we acknowledge that everyone is bound by the limitations of being human. We are forever inside a human suit that we can't zip off, and so understanding your own sense of personal psychology and biology are of the utmost importance if you truly care about bridging the gap and communicating with others who are different.

Our premise is that YOU—whether or not you're the manager, decision-maker, or boss—can be an impactful leader in nearly all your professional relationships by:

1. Taking personal responsibility for how you show up in the relationship and/or in each interaction.
2. Using curiosity as a reliable tool and intentional filter for how you listen, speak, and engage in relationship building.
3. Communicating openly so that all parties can speak their minds and truths to find a way forward.

You will be able to apply and integrate these tangible skills with your work colleagues (and beyond) to bridge gaps of differences and perspectives.

Why do we believe so strongly?

Because we have witnessed time and time again the power of regular people showing up differently to communicate better. Our work as trainers and coaches has been vast but always singularly focused on accelerating performance by bridging gaps and communicating effectively. From working with CEOs, boards of directors, employees, and teams across Fortune 500 companies and smaller organizations, we have helped equip them with tools that transform their work and increase productivity and workplace satisfaction.

You will read many stories and case studies based on our work with actual clients that will resonate with you. You may find yourself jeering or cheering as you engage with their stories. And since we aren't in the business of airing people's dirty laundry, we have, in honor of our clients, changed their names, gender, industry, and more, to illustrate the very real frustrations, fears, meltdowns—and wins—that they have experienced.

So, whether you're a founder, in the C-suite, a manager, realtor, graphic designer, educator, headhunter, executive director, pastor, fundraiser, secretary, entrepreneur—or any of the millions of roles to play in an organization—all of it is applicable because we each play an important function. All of us need meaningful relationships with people who are different from us because that is where collaboration, growth, and expansion happens.

And us authors are no exception to that rule.

We couldn't be more different from the outside looking in; we, Jennifer and Katie, appear like different sides of a coin: Republican/Democrat; Christian/spiritual explorer; executive/ creative; conservative/liberal; country/rock 'n' roll; polished/ tattooed; and upper class/working class. From the inside looking out, we are two entrepreneurs who desire to work for purpose and prosperity. We've grown into "work-wives," which is our way of defining our relationship. It's a "marriage" with a lot at stake. Our open communication methods have allowed us to traverse hard stuff and real tensions that arise nearly daily in this crazy world. The tools, skills, and strategies in this book allow us consistently to disengage from toxic rhetoric (internal and external) and miscommunication that threatens our work.

We wish the same outcome for you—in your business, your work relationships, and in your community—because quality communication is the lynchpin of success and it begins with YOU.

You always have a choice, and therefore, power is always in your hands.

YOUR BRAIN UNDER PRESSURE
AMY and the Hijack

Claire barges into our coworking space one afternoon, pulls her laptop out of her purse, and throws it on the couch. "One of you needs to sit by me as I send this email 'cause I'm done! They don't get it. They'll never get it. I guess I have to spell it out for them, one last time." Her face is pinched in anger, and she definitely doesn't look like the beautiful Claire we have come to adore.

Katie smirks, "In an email, huh? Yea. That seems . . . smart. Maybe a text message with emojis would be better."

"Shut up!" Claire shoots back, sits on the couch, and opens her laptop.

Jennifer nods. "Well, hello Claire. Lovely to see you."

Claire pats the empty seat next to her on the couch. "OK. Who is going to sit here and write this for me? I'm out of things to say, so I hope you ladies have some language because I'm going to explode."

Claire manages a theater company, along with twelve volunteer board members from the community who are also, collectively, her "boss." Imagine having a "they" as your boss . . . twelve different people with diverse communication styles, expectations, and needs. Claire can handle it though—she's feisty, wicked smart, and quick as a hummingbird. As a community leader, she is accomplished, experienced, and admired. However, when she doesn't get what she wants . . . Claire morphs into a meltdown monster. When Claire is like this, it takes a day or so for her to return to the creative, good-hearted Claire that we—and most people—know and like.

Unfortunately, though, time moves quick in Claire's busy world of deadlines, rehearsals, fundraising, and performances. She doesn't have a day to lose, and she really needs an engaged board to keep the theater thriving. We need to quickly get her into a better headspace so that she can go back to her board and communicate her goals and needs better without burning all her bridges.

In our line of work, we see a lot of Claires, normal, hard-working, and stressed-out people who, in times of pressure, want to know: *What should I say and how should I say it?*

We know . . . we know . . . everyone wants the quick fix. If it were that easy, we'd hand out scripts and send people on their merry way to "fix" their professional relationships. It doesn't work that way. The path to becoming a great communicator doesn't really have anything to do with your vocabulary and/or how you speak.

In this chapter, and the following three, you'll learn how your biology and psychology create certain conditions that critically impact how you communicate and maneuver within both work and personal relationships—especially ones that are stressful. Understanding how the brain, body, and mind work *against* your efforts to communicate allows you to know what you have to disrupt and combat before you have any chance of bridging the gap. We will share with you memorable analogies and teach tangible strategies that immediately improve how you show up in conversations and moments that are important. This work *is* the necessary foundation to build better relationships, improve communication, and increase your ability to collaborate effectively.

THE SINGLE KEY FACTOR THAT YOU NEED TO BRIDGE THE GAP: PSYCHOLOGICAL FLEXIBILITY

You're probably like the average American, spending roughly 47.5 hours a week at work.[1] You likely spend more time with colleagues than with your friends and family, and even experience some of your most meaningful relationships inside your career. According to one study, staying engaged and performing well at work is *directly* tied to the closeness that you feel with coworkers. Nearly 40 percent of people said that their coworkers were the top reason that they loved working for a particular company, and 66 percent of those relationships positively impact their focus and productivity.[2]

We're assuming that you value your precious time as much as we do. So, if you're investing that much time—47.5 hours per week—into your career and away from your family and friends, don't you want it to be somewhat enjoyable, too? Claire does. Anne from Chapter 1 does. We're pretty sure that Dr. Malcolm and Claire's all-volunteer board does, too.

Everyone wants good relationships—even people who seem to sabotage them.

So, what is it at the core of an individual that creates healthy and happy relationships? It's not being born with charisma or charm. It's not being an extrovert who loves people. It's not even about having great communication or relationship-building skills.

The Journal of Contextual Behavioral Science concluded, after reviewing 174 studies that engaged approximately 44,000 individuals, that there was only ONE key factor that really mattered in healthy relationships: *psychological flexibility*.[3]

That means that at least one person in the relationship chooses to bridge the gap of their differences, especially in moments of pressure and stress, by being flexible.

A psychologically flexible person is someone who has both an attitude and a skillset that allows them to be curious about a wide range of experiences without feeling judgment, rejection, or discomfort. A psychologically flexible person may hear or witness something new and become curious about what they don't know that they didn't know. They choose to listen, ask questions, and explore new thinking instead of becoming suspicious, defensive, or stuck in their ways of thinking about something. Consider the following example:

Claire has psychological flexibility, or she wouldn't even be qualified to run a theater company. As a former actress herself, she understands the human condition, can inhabit different characters, and can suspend her own personality to make those roles believably come to life for an audience.

However, when Claire is triggered and under pressure—she isn't Claire. She is another beast all together. She becomes hijacked by a habitually wired response in her brain to behave poorly, especially when she is met with a board that struggles to engage as a team and accomplish important tasks for the organization. It makes sense because there is a lot at stake. If she and the board can't strategically communicate to collaborate and execute on their strategic plan and duties, the theater will be shuttered permanently.

Truly, Claire is under immense pressure. Pressure to succeed. Pressure to sell tickets and run shows and fundraise to pay actors, staff, herself, and the rent. She is under pressure to delegate tasks to her board and motivate them to work as a team while also trying to please them as her employers. In addition, she has a full personal life with its own set of pressures.

When Claire blows up like this, she struggles to be psychologically flexible. Her relationships and communication skills are subpar. She says (or emails): "It is my way or the highway, this is how the theater has always done things—so step up or ship out." She becomes unwilling to bend to their suggestions of other ways to accomplish their goals. She denies her board a safe space to ask questions or share concerns because she is defensive. This inflexibility can also show up as being dogmatic and boxing people into labels and roles. For instance, in her frustration, she transforms her board of caring volunteers into villains holding her back or sabotaging her efforts. She becomes rigid.

Do you know what happens to trees if they don't bend in a storm? They break.

If Claire doesn't disrupt her reaction to the pressure she's feeling, then that email she wants to send could get her fired—and that's not even the real problem. Her firing would negatively impact all the actors, volunteers, patrons, and the community. What an avoidable disaster.

How Psychologically Flexible Are You?

Let's flip this psychological flexibility stuff back to you. Are there moments when you:

- Feel like you're the most open person in the world?
- Are able to hear new ideas and perspectives even when they don't match yours?
- Are able to suspend your criticism or doubts for people to be able to express something that you've never heard of, don't believe in, or don't understand?

Vice versa, are there times when you simply cannot—cannot hear any more information, pushback, ideas, or questions? Are there instances where you draw the line and stop trying to even get along or bridge the gap with someone who you can't understand, like, or respect?

Of course, people are *whole* people—even at work—meaning that we all experience highs and lows. Many of us carry our emotions into conference rooms and offices, whether or not we're aware of them. Can you identify a pattern to when you behave a certain way? Also, is there a pattern of WHO you behave this way with? Are there certain triggers that hijack you from being your best professional self? And is it really the other person—or group's—fault when you're in a reactive state? Something happened that sent Claire into a tizzy. Either a board committee didn't follow through with their duties, which impacts her timelines and funding streams, or, more likely (because we've known Claire a long time), a certain board member probably requested a document or a spreadsheet to gain clarity on the data or duties again, and they probably asked in a way that rubbed her wrong (cause she's likely provided this information to them before) and now she's fuming mad and defensive at not just one member but all of them.

Claire needs to get back to being flexible.

Can you view psychological flexibility as an asset that is sitting, sometimes untapped, inside your toolbox of communication and relationship strategies? Even when you're on fire and beyond irritated? Because that's the trick. We believe that psychological flexibility can be expressed, even when it's somewhat forced.

The COVID-19 global pandemic proved to be a great example of how businesses that embodied psychological flexibility were able to reposition themselves and stay open. For example, some owners of restaurants from traditionally dine-in-only establishments were able to quickly reposition themselves when take-out meals started to gain traction. One of our clients, the owner of a chain of local upscale breakfast/lunch restaurants, relayed to us how challenged they felt when they could no longer seat customers in their luxurious booths with decadent meals by their head chef. Plus, they didn't have outdoor space to set up for social distancing.

But instead of closing up shop and laying off workers, they challenged their long-held beliefs about service and the dining experience to come up with solutions to keep revenue flowing. At first, they did the typical take-out orders, but when revenue flattened, they quickly found a new value proposition against the hundreds of other "take-out" competitors: they pivoted to selling family meal kits with cooking instructions and free online videos of their chef and his crew teaching favorites off their menu—and those sold like hotcakes. They became so popular, they eventually created four different subscription boxes for their customers, which in turn helped them anticipate and plan for revenue amid all the uncertainty.

If you had told this restaurant group that they would eventually run an upscale at-home meal kit dinner service with instructional videos about how to cook and serve their top-secret signature recipes . . . they would have rolled their eyes. That eyeroll equates to saying: *That's not who we are, that's not our business model, that's not something we could ever consider.* Without psychological flexibility, they probably would have folded under the fear that they couldn't possibly give up their "secret sauce" to the masses through meal kits and online videos. Instead, they worked through the uncertainty and fear, bridged their own gap, and increased revenue by 13 percent.

Another client talked to us about the critical nature of hiring and training psychologically flexible sales leaders in their medical sales business. Given that accounts were competitive and often hard to "win," the difference between success and failure for these salespeople was all about how they bounced back from being told "no." For those who viewed it as *That client is not ready for me,*

YET, a rejection didn't stop them from going forward and potentially revisiting that client later.

The thing about psychological flexibility is that in moments when you are under pressure and feeling stuck, rigid, or similar to Claire, or *just plain done*, you struggle to access it. So, you need to learn how to get it back. That is why this quick primer on how the brain learns and engages with stress and new information will help set you up for greater flexibility in how you approach people when under pressure.

MEETING EMOTIONAL NEEDS HELPS BRIDGE THE GAP

Believe or not, humans are predictable. You are predictable. Why? Because you and every human on the planet were born with a set of physical needs and emotional needs that need to be met, nearly at all times, or you don't perform optimally. This is universally acknowledged and often is taught through psychologist Dr. Abraham Maslow's Hierarchy of Needs, depicted as a triangle with five layers from a seminal paper titled "A Theory of Human Motivation."[4] His work illuminates that these needs provide a motivational foundation for human behavior.

Your physical needs are shelter, sustenance, sleep, and sanitation. In our modern professional world, in first-world countries, most people have those covered. It's emotional needs that need tending to in our relationships. They are:

1. To be understood
2. To be accepted
3. To be valued

At all times, you are seeking to meet your physical and emotional needs, whether or not you are aware of it. A key contention that surprises many people is that your emotional needs are just as important—if not more—than your physical ones.[5]

Emotional needs are often so powerful that we often see them playing out in work relationships where a leader, employee, or client has no idea that they are being demonstrated.

Think about that person at work who overstates their point, with multiple examples, and maybe even repeats what they say over and over again. That person may have an emotional need to be understood and is therefore using many different (long-winded) ways to express their thoughts and ideas.

And what about that new hire who is feeling awkward and a bit shy during their first month at work and they have asked you to teach them the ropes of how your organization celebrates birthdays, holidays, and engages in team-building experiences. They are hoping to be accepted into the culture of the organization and play by its unspoken rules.

For example, a work colleague who is constantly seeking that "attaboy" or awards and accolades is possibly playing out in front of you his lack of feeling valued (either at home, work, in personal or professional relationships).

What emotional needs are at stake for Claire in this moment? Claire clearly isn't feeling understood, accepted, or valued by her board in this moment and her reaction is to dominate, control, and lambaste the board into submission. Which will make her feel better—but only for a moment.

▶ The Big Aha! ◀

When there is a gap in the relationship, it likely means that emotional needs aren't being met on both sides. That's the gap we need to close. And it takes someone with psychological flexibility to step up and move closer to the other person in that relationship to meet those fundamental core needs.

If you're struggling to understand, like, or respect the other—you aren't meeting their emotional needs to be understood, accepted, or valued. And you likely feel this way because they aren't meeting your same emotional needs. Exhibit 2.1 illustrates this point.

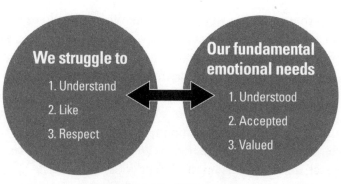

EXHIBIT 2.1 The Bridge to Gap

So, as much as you'd like a quick-fix solution like Claire—
*What do I say and how do I say it? Let me just write this email or
text and tell them exactly what I think so I can shut this down*—it
doesn't work. Words won't fill the gap until much later. It's how
you show up differently to connect across the gap to collaborate
that moves the relationship forward before you have any shot at
communication.

For Claire, she needs to disrupt her reaction, put the laptop
away, and reclaim her energy to approach the board anew.

MANAGING PRESSURE AND DEALING WITH "AMY"

How do you manage pressure? How do you behave when stress,
anxiety, fear, shame, worry, awkwardness, doubt, panic, and any
extreme emotion (even joy) shows up?

What is your response when someone in the company passive-
aggressively shames you for not making the sales pipeline quota?
(Do you feel your value has been undermined, threatening how
you are accepted in the team?)

What about when the new client that promised to sign the
contract but didn't come through and now your entire quarter's
revenue projection is shot, and your manager doesn't understand
what happened and is pissed? (You likely feel misunderstood and
possibly like a failure.)

Or perhaps you are in a one-to-one with your client and they ask you a question about the metrics, and you know you should have prepared for it, but you answer with a lame and inadequate reply because you were tired last night from being up with your teenage daughter who was crying all night long. (You now feel insecure, wondering about your own value and your ability to perform your role for your company).

We refer to all these feelings as *pressure* to simplify the complex spectrum of emotions and reactions that hijack your best efforts to be present, curious, and connective. Pressure is anything that pushes you into a reactive state, impeding your ability to communicate and collaborate.

Pressure is constant. It never goes away.

The issue is that you've often been sold that there is a magic cure to eliminate or nearly erase the discomforts of pressure. It's natural to want to bypass the difficulty, awkwardness, and irritation of pressure . . . but it's here to stay. You probably have experiences like Claire, where you'd rather avoid face-to-face conversations about what's really happening and send emails or text messages instead. Or worse, ignore the dilemma, play the martyr, and just "do it yourself."

Mindfulness guru and researcher Jon Kabat-Zinn said: "You can't stop the waves, but you can learn to surf."[6] This is a big deal because if you embrace that pressure and reactivity is natural then perhaps you won't fight or work to avoid it. So when someone like Claire comes at you, you'll have more understanding about their reactivity. And over time, you'll become stronger and more confident at handling your relationships and communication when it counts.

This is Jedi-level stuff because it's coupling personal awareness with personal responsibility. We're asking you to step up and defuse your negative tendencies before they mess up your positive intentions to have great working relationships.

It's the difference maker. So how does it work? What is driving you to feel these emotions and react?

Every day, you consciously and unconsciously navigate pressure that shows up in your body, which stems from an autopilot response within the brain. Your brain is committed to a learned pattern of behavior that reliably keeps you safe—at all costs—when threats and pressure arrive, whether or not you are in actual danger. The auto-response is often referred to as "wiring,"[7] similar to how a car works. For instance, if you want to drive, you turn the key, press the gas, and steer, accelerating and braking along the trip. This only reliably happens if the wiring works in coordination with the engine, the wheels, fuel, brakes, chemicals, and many other complex machines within the car's system.

People are no different.

The brain creates reliable and habitual behavior patterns based on your past experiences[8] with pressure. And since we live in the pressure cooker of life—employee drama, traffic, divorce, aging, pandemics, social media dynamics, keeping up with the Joneses—everyone you encounter, talk to, and collaborate with is experiencing their own unique sense of pressure, too.

Now maybe you, like most folks we know, believe that you're fully in charge of your behavior, that you can muster enough willpower to change anything . . . and that's an adorable assumption. The truth is that you are—and aren't—fully in charge of your machinery, chemicals, and wiring. In addition, culture, your family of origin, generational differences, socioeconomics, and other factors affect your behavior. These determinants though are often, frustratingly, out of your control, too. This is why change is difficult. Your brain works against your change efforts because of deeply embedded, habitual wiring coupled with the overwhelming impact of cultural and societal determinants. If it were easy to change behavior, there would be no diet, self-help, psychology, or other industries generating billions of dollars.

In addition, you have an invisible and highly impactful "frenemy" riding shotgun with you at all times. Understanding, valuing, and respecting all the different ways this invisible force impacts your life and others is a significant gamechanger.

Meet AMY.

At the base of the brain is the *AMYgdala* (Ah-Mig-dahlah). We chose to personify this small group of cells as "AMY" for short because it's been a proven way[9] to illustrate "her" impact on us. "She" is responsible for fight, flight, or freeze in nearly all living creatures, with a few exceptions (jellyfish and snakes, for example). AMY belongs to the least-evolved section of the brain, and her primary function is to keep us alive. She does this by scanning for threats, which can be actual or perceived.[10] For example, in the modern world, AMY struggles to tell the difference between being held at gunpoint versus being shamed by a relative at Thanksgiving dinner or by a colleague in a staff meeting.

When actual survival issues arise, like being held hostage in a bank robbery, AMY reacts quickly. First, she alerts us to find other people, unconsciously asking: "Who's here to help me?" Then, if she doesn't feel safe, she pushes us to run, hide, fight, freeze, or defend to protect ourselves and resources. She takes up a very small space in the brain, about the size of an almond, but she holds the heavyweight champion title of "the Pressure Queen." She keeps our instincts alert, keeps us alive, and for that we are grateful.

AMY is not so helpful, though, when we face perceived threats, like:

- Having tough conversations
- Being bullied or shamed either directly or passive-aggressively
- Answering tons of questions about our thought process, ideas, or "why" we do things a certain way
- Fessing up to being wrong
- Losing our jobs
- Experiencing unanticipated change

AMY orchestrates a primal state of being, pushing us toward fear and negativity, doubt and pessimism, anger and anxiety, and worry and judgment—all in the name of "protection." Essentially, whenever we start feeling reactive and defensive . . . AMY has crashed the party.

She does this by spewing cortisol, epinephrine, catecholamine, testosterone, and norepinephrine whenever she identifies anything that threatens her kingdom of safety. This *chemical cocktail* is a mix of hormones, neurotransmitters, and chemicals that flood the brain, activating a habitual behavior pattern. When this cocktail hits, we rarely feel safe to engage in psychological flexibility. We go rigid.[11]

Think About Your Own Reactions to Various Situations

Let's run a short experiment. Please remember one of the following scenarios. Choose only one, please. Take one full minute and recall that moment. Go there. Feel it.

- You got back your 360 annual review. The feedback reveals some hard things to swallow.
- You are driving home after receiving your bonus check and excited to tell your family and maybe buy that car you have been pining after.
- You just walked out of a one-to-one where your boss let you know you missed the mark on the last project you led and you're kind of surprised at her harsh comments.
- You sent an email to the wrong person with sensitive company information and panic. This could be trouble.
- Your coworker hands you a greeting card with handwritten words of acknowledgment about how you inspire them, and you had no idea they thought this about you.
- A name on your phone appears and you're filled with dread. You clench your jaw deciding whether or not to answer.
- Someone likes all your pictures from your vacation on social media.
- You have to present a slide deck to a group of investors, and you clam up and freeze.

Revisiting any of those scenarios caused some kind of biological reaction in your body. Did you feel it? Your neurochemistry went into overdrive when you started to relive the scenario.[12] Whether or not you felt positive or negative, or high or low, something showed up that began governing you, how you felt, what you thought, or why you reacted in a certain way.

Your communication and relationship skills are always impacted by your neurochemistry. And these skills exist in a part of your brain called the neocortex, which is the largest, most complex and evolved part. The neocortex provides you with your high-function processing and cognition, things such as language, logic, and creativity. Within the neocortex is the prefrontal cortex which gives us curiosity to explore our world. The prefrontal cortex is a giant squishy pink mass behind your forehead.

The neocortex and prefrontal cortex's machinations coordinate all of the above into something referred to as your *executive function*.[13] AMY halts or impedes the wonderful gifts of your executive function when she spews her chemical cocktail as pressure hits. She releases the stress hormone—cortisol—and that can flood your pink prefrontal cortex like a dark cloud. It can take up to 26 hours for cortisol to lessen its impact and leave the body, impairing your executive function *the whole time*.[14]

YOU don't have that time to lose. How many times are you stressed out at work in a week? In a day? Twenty-six hours is a full day, plus some! That's a long time to wait to return to full functionality.

For example, one of our clients, a CEO/founder, was heading into a three-day strategic retreat that he had spent lots of time and money preparing for. He was geared up, having planned with facilitators high-energy sessions with lots of activities surrounding a new product. His small but mighty team was scheduled to meet up at noon in Lake Tahoe. By 1 p.m., a member of the team had not arrived because of a car accident that they witnessed. While that person was physically safe, the impact of the collision left him emotionally raw. In addition, another member of the team arrived late as well and was in a very vulnerable place, acknowledging that she had just been served divorce papers. Of the five people in the "room," there were only three brains ready to work.

The CEO/founder gave us a call and we talked about what to do to both support his goals and where his team was at. Wisely, he decided to put people before product and canceled the first afternoon of the retreat, asking that each member do what would best serve them and to show up ready to work the next morning. That small amount of space and grace he offered was a strategic move because he realized that the important decisions they needed to be making in those first sessions would create a domino effect for the entire launch. He wasn't just being kind. He needed a unified team with five brains in a clean and creative state to communicate and collaborate.

To top it all off, AMY also unleashes habitual reactions within other parts of the brain, which impacts all our biological systems. She is part of the limbic system, which is responsible for pupil dilation, heart rate, and how much we sweat. The limbic system part of our brain also processes feelings, emotions, moods, experiences, and information. The limbic system "files" all that data as memories,[15] transforming them into stories that become something meaningful to you (which you'll explore in the next chapter). Ultimately, this is where you make sense of the world—determining how it works and how you belong within it. And when AMY's chemical cocktails flood your limbic system, your behavior, choices, and level of curiosity are impacted—meaning unconsciously you will either seek to connect with or disconnect from people and ideas that threaten how you view the world.

▶ Another Big Aha! ◀

You're most likely to pull away from someone who doesn't share your worldview, generational thinking, way of doing things, communication style, and more. If you truly want to bridge the gap, then you have to move closer to them, and that is something most people don't want to do. The most successful people in life move closer, not farther away from, others. And that requires you to have psychological flexibility when hijacked by AMY.

Did you ever play with a finger trap when you were little? You know that little braided cylinder where you stick a finger in both ends and when you try to pull your fingers out the braid tightens and your fingers become stuck? The only way to get out of the finger trap is to push both fingers toward each other, eliminating the gap between them. Once you do this, the braid expands, and your fingers are free!

Same thing happens in sticky relationships. When you tussle, fight, argue, cajole, convince, ignore, or just plain struggle to communicate with another at work, you both tend to pull away . . . becoming even more trapped and stuck in a relationship that isn't serving the work. When you're in the finger trap with another, like Claire and her board, or like Anne and Dr. Malcolm, someone has to move closer first. The key is to lean in, get curious, and try to connect better to the person that is troubling you—and often that means meeting their emotional needs—conveying that you understand them, accept their point of view even if you don't agree, and value their contribution. That's when the finger trap ceases to have any power over you both.

Very few of us are aware of the powerful grip that AMY has over our best intentions. When it comes to the quality of your relationships and how you show up to connect, consider that other people are also contending with their own habitual reactions, neurochemistry, and AMY.

The good news is that you can do this! Even with AMY, your brain is perpetually evolving and malleable.[16] More importantly, your brain is shaped, wired, and then continuously rewired[17] in response to how you manage pressure and AMY over time. For example:

> Claire is managing her AMY and the accompanying chaotic emotions.
>
> Jennifer sat next to her on the couch, took the laptop out of Claire's hands and closed it. "Are you here or is AMY?"
>
> Claire sighed. "AMY."
>
> "I read a great quote this morning from Dale Carnegie," Katie said. "He said, 'If you want to gather honey, don't kick over the beehive.'"
>
> "Claire, is it possible for us to take a moment before writing that email?" Jennifer asked. "Can we talk about what happened and then create a plan for how you will engage them to action?"
>
> "Yes, please. But first, lemme tell you what Brad said . . . ," Claire responds, and is off down her rabbit hole, venting and releasing pressure so that she can return to functional. And that's just fine. It's how she copes and processes. We are patient and present with her as she empties a full cup of her thoughts and feelings. Eventually she starts to consciously embrace having psychological flexibility and chooses a careful response with clear communication over a messy reaction.

We implore you to see AMY as a tool of awareness to change and embrace your psychological flexibility, especially in moments where you feel like bridging the gap is impossible.

REFLECTION QUESTIONS

- Consider your psychological flexibility. What do you notice about yourself?
- What are the contributing factors to your inflexiblity?
- How do you show up when you're under pressure?
- How do others show up with you when they seem under pressure?

ACTION ITEM
The Choice: Response Over Reaction

The next time you feel pressure build up in your body as frustration, rage, annoyance, or irritation, identify immediately if AMY's chemical cocktail is hijacking your communication, problem-solving, and decision-making skills. Choose to suspend your reaction during her hijack, which will lessen the potential twenty-six hours that you could lose to her clouding your executive function. We will give you on-the-spot strategies in Chapter 5. Ultimately, awareness is both an aspiration and a choice—it invites you to show up and respond differently. Let go of your need to control an outcome until you have more clarity.

JOIN THE CONVERSATION ONLINE
#responseoverreaction

YOUR MIND UNDER PRESSURE
An Inner Narrator and a Kaleidoscope

We have a friend who taught us a skill that, originally, made us roll our eyes. Yet it's a genius strategy that, while kind of silly, actually works to supersize your psychological flexibility and help you bridge the gap in work relationships where you struggle to connect, communicate, and collaborate.

Francisco is a 55-year-old Mexican American man who everybody admires and likes. He transforms nearly all his professional relationships into authentic friendships, which is not easy considering that he works in a politicized position as the executive director of a "property business improvement district." His job is to convene an association of diverse people that oversee a pot of public and private funds to create bustling, vibrant places where people will spend money to shop, eat, or gather. At any given moment, he is bridging the gap between what business owners, school officials, government leaders, and residents want to see happen in their neighborhoods. His job is always public-facing and highly contentious, so his communication skills have to be polished at all times.

People trust—and follow—Francisco.

That's not luck. He has invested time in getting to know people at a deeper level than their professional functions. This can make things tricky given his role. Nearly every week, he's caught between "friends" who are bickering over the association's direction or on how to spend the money. In these rough mediation-type situations, he often refers to himself as "Switzerland" (because of how this country has historically practiced neutrality during times of war). We've observed three crucial things that Francisco does when he acts like "Switzerland":

1. His perspective is that people aren't that different. They all want the same fundamental outcome—a better quality of life. People are simply arguing about the resources and how to achieve it and in doing so lose sight of their shared goal and commonalities.

2. He is often able to suspend his own agenda, preferences, and perspectives. He can disrupt his own triggers and emotions. He explained once that he carries those feelings with him in a metaphorical backpack and intentionally leaves it outside the door in any of these conversations where collaboration between people is key.

3. He commits to caring about what both parties want while strategically moving them to a place where they can have a shared perspective, along with a common goal that, if accomplished, will be valuable to both parties.

Clearly Francisco is an expert at bridging perspectives and moving people to action.

If we're going to make a case study out of Francisco, then let's be clear about what he is NOT. He doesn't wear a cape and fly like Superman. He's not a Zen master. He isn't immune to pressure, nor absolved of his own AMY hijack, either. Just like you, he can't zip off his human suit. He has a very full life, schedule, and responsibilities. He is humble. He isn't supported by a large staff or big budget—his team is small, and their budget is shoestring. He experiences stress, disappointments, and awkwardness like the rest of us leaders and worker bees. Just like you and me, he struggles to understand, like, and respect some people.

Yet Francisco has something remarkable, something beyond psychological flexibility . . . and that's what we want to understand better.

What tangible lessons can we take away from him, especially if we don't share his background or personality?

We pestered him to tell us what makes him, him. Frankly, he couldn't really articulate anything helpful. He'd say things like, "I like people, I guess. They don't scare me when they're upset." So, we followed him around for a few weeks, shadowing his meetings and watching him interact. And, then, he caught our attention when he shared with us his Monday morning ritual. He talks to himself, out loud, alone in the car on his commute. He reflects on his behavior from the previous week and talks about himself in the third person. We asked him to tell us what kinds of things he says, out loud, to himself. They go something like this:

- "Francisco really wants the mural project completed but it's at least two more months away from completion. Patience was hard for Francisco last week because everyone wants to know when the murals will be displayed, but the artists don't have enough supplies to finish. He can focus his efforts on supporting the artists."
- "Francisco felt ignored when Amber took over the committee meeting and ran out of time to let him present his information or slides. He can ask Amber to email the information to the team this afternoon, instead. No biggie."
- "Francisco was a little too distracted in that meeting by his text messages with the mayor and missed something important that was said. Francisco, keep your phone in your briefcase."
- "Last week, Francisco told himself that story about Julius, again. The same old one that insists Julius is on a mission to squash Measure F and the ½ cent sales tax effort and bad-mouth Francisco's team. That's not entirely true, Francisco. Julius wants to make sure that if Measure F passes then the extra ½ cent will invest in infrastructure that Francisco and his team don't find necessary. The truth is that Francisco doesn't really like spending time with Julius because of his overbearing tone and bravado. Julius is a man fighting hard for his business and customers. Francisco and the team have to keep finding common ground to defuse Julius's tendency to 'come out all guns blazing.' Francisco won't give up—this is too important for the community."

Yep, in private, Francisco talks to himself in the third person as a way to review and prepare for the week ahead. And it's a brilliant strategy that we believe is intrinsic to his communication and relationship skills.

We asked him how he learned to do this and why. He basically said this:

> As a young immigrant to this country, I've often been very lonely. When I was learning English, people didn't really understand me. Some people didn't like me, even though I was trying to learn. I felt judged and caught between two worlds—the worlds of America and Mexico and the world of what I wanted to be and who I had yet to become. I had to become my own friend and coach myself or I was going to lose hope and have to go home with nothing. I couldn't do that to my family or to myself. Today, I don't have a traditional boss giving me feedback so that I can learn. I have always watched myself as an outsider and I try to self-correct as best I can.

Whoa. That's some high-level awareness and perhaps born out of his needs as a young immigrant. His emotional needs to be understood, accepted, and valued were not being met in his experience, so he found a way to meet his own in order to work and belong in the United States. Now it makes sense to us why Francisco turns professional relationships into friendships—he doesn't want to be lonely! *Francisco bridged his own gap.*

More importantly, what we can learn from Francisco is how he practices not only *psychological flexibility* but also *psychological distance.* By speaking in the third person to himself as he drives into work each Monday, he creates intentional space between his ego—that powerful spirit stewing inside every human that often takes things too personally—and the myriad of thoughts in his mind. While it may seem silly and something you may scoff at, it works and allows Francisco to show up "clean" in his interactions—not tainted by an agenda to be right and exercise power over another in the pursuit of winning—and that's why people trust, like, and admire Francisco, because he can expansively think beyond his ego.

Let's flip it back to you:

- Are you aware of how your ego interferes with your ability to bridge the gap, especially when you're under pressure and working with someone with whom you struggle?
- Are you aware of how your thoughts might be turning sour?
- Have you ever placed your own self at a psychological distance as a way to understand your ego?
- Are you ready to perform mind control over yourself to better your communication and relationships?

IMPACT OF YOUR EGO AND MIND

Everyone has an ego, which is truly the part of your human suit that you can't zip off.

Ego is most often defined as the view that a person has of themselves, often elevating oneself with importance and esteem. When under pressure, your ego often takes things personally and turns you into a beast that defends itself by insisting to be seen as smart, clever, powerful, unique, and correct in nearly every interaction.

Remember Claire in the last chapter? Her ego was on fire because she had taken something personally from a board member. When she burst into our office, she was triggered by AMY's chemical cocktail AND her ego was looking to be justified. It was AMY and her ego that wanted to send the email to the board, with language that showed her board how her perspective was the powerful one to obey.

Your ego can get the best of you. When under its spell, you tend to communicate in ways that turn people off, which impacts how they want to connect and collaborate with you. Because who wants to work with someone who is always about *me, me, me?*

We suspect that Francisco's Monday morning ritual of self-reflection and psychological distancing in the third person helps him navigate the space between what his ego wants and what he actually needs to accomplish to bridge the gap. He exercises control over his thoughts, allowing him to show up clean in any room, any time, with nearly anyone. When Francisco comes with clean energy—he is open, present, and able to connect, have curiosity about various perspectives, and navigate conversations that might be uncomfortable. If Francisco were Claire from Chapter 2, he would likely forgo the email and call an in-person meeting with the board to determine the disconnect between their duties and performance. He'd show up with a smile, leave his metaphorical backpack of egotistical junk outside the door, and create a safe space for dialogue to hear how the needs of the board aren't being met without shaming them or feeling ashamed.

Either way, both Claire and Francisco are under pressure to perform. It's how they respond, rather than react, that makes the difference.

In the last chapter, you learned how your brain reacts to external pressure, proving that your biology heavily impacts how you show up to connect, communicate, and collaborate. Let's learn about the role your mind plays in relationship building and communication.

First, is there even a difference between your brain and your mind?

Yes and no. They are interconnected.

Your brain is made up of organs, tissues, and chemicals that coordinate your bodily and executive function. Your mind houses the *invisible stuff*, a.k.a., your internal world. Your mind processes what you see, feel, hear, and experience into thoughts. Your brain and mind work in synchronicity to create your conscious experience.[1] Together, they bridge the gap between your external world of experiences and your internal world of feeling and thinking about those experiences. This crucial interplay between the brain and mind is how you shape your sense of reality.[2] You create stories about what happened and why. The stories you tell yourself over and over become your perspective about how the world works.

Your brain and mind never stop crafting stories because humans are meaning-making and judgment-assessing machines. When you go to sleep, the limbic part of your brain continues working, all night, "filing away" the experiences of your day. At the same time, your mind processes those experiences into stories that inform your decision-making when you are awake.[3]

Think of having an internal filing cabinet: the brain creates the file, and the mind creates the label. When information comes to you that is familiar and that you have already assessed and judged, your brain and mind have a story about it already and can quickly file the information away. Easy peasy.

However, when you come across a new piece of information—a person, a story, or an idea that you don't necessarily understand, like, or even have reference for—your brain and mind ask: *What is this new stuff? How will it impact me? Is it a threat?* In that place of confusion, you might resist being open, curious, and connective with what's unfamiliar.

Here's an example. You're in charge of the desserts for the office holiday party. You've done this for the past four years and take great pride in bringing the most delectable goodies for your colleagues to enjoy. You do all the baking yourself—spending the year collecting recipes on your Pinterest board. It's quite an act of love, and everyone in the office knows that the dessert table is *your thing*. Among all the chatter about what decadent surprises you'll bring this year, the recent new hire, Jackie, has indicated that she doesn't eat sugar, carbs, and is vegan. "That'll be a challenge for you!" She says, laughing in good clean fun. In front of her and your colleagues, you say, "Of course! I'll knock it out of the park like I always do." Inside, however, you're not that amused and feel a slight panic.

Your mind immediately latched onto the word *vegan*. You have not had good experiences with vegan food or culture. And if we're being honest, you struggle with people who are health conscious, because you are not. It is not a part of your story or value system. Based on your lived experiences, you believe that people should eat whatever they want. You don't understand why some people punish themselves over the yummy stuff in life: frosting, butter, sugar. And when they bring up how bad those ingredients are for the human body, you feel judged and annoyed. Vegans, in particular, are judgy and not your people, or at least that's what you have told yourself, over and over again, based on the information in your file about them.

The next morning, Jackie arrives bright-eyed at your desk with a slip of paper. "If you've never had vegan cupcakes, you're missing out. They are way more delicious than the real ones. John let me know that you're a fabulous baker and if you're up for it this is my favorite devil's food cupcake recipe. If you want, I can bring them to the party, but I don't want to step on your toes. So, if you want to give this recipe a go, awesome; if you don't, I can do it!"

She places the recipe on top of your keyboard. Her smile is as wide as the Mississippi river . . . a river you'd like to drown her in. You muster your best smile back and glance at the recipe, which has some ingredients you've never baked with before. A sour voice inside says, *Where the hell am I gonna even find this stuff?*

Jackie has positive intentions. She is trying to connect with you through your baking . . . while also maintaining one of her values (being health conscious and vegan). This is the gap. One of the things you likely value is showing people you care by treating them. Furthermore, you're applauded for your treats. Every time a colleague enjoys your blueberry cheesecake and sings your praises in the office, you feel amazing because all of your emotional needs to be understood, liked, and respected are met.

Jackie has challenged this with her request to be cared for—by you—in the same way. She wants you to bake her something that you're not familiar baking. And furthermore, it challenges your story about vegans. Likely, you're missing Jackie's good intentions, soured by this internal thinking, *just another overbearing health nut shoving their fanatic ideas on people.*

"Thanks, Jackie, I'll try my best." You reply with a drop of sarcasm.

She hears it.

"Sorry, I didn't mean to put something on you—I'm more than happy to bring the cupcakes myself. I get it! Veganism isn't for everyone." She smiles back, softly. You can see that she is a tad hurt, but trying not to show it.

"Oh no . . . , I'll do it! Will be good for me to try." You now feel guilty for showing a bit of your disdain and agree to try the recipe.

"Thanks. Let me know if you need any help. I appreciate you." She smiles.

You're still not happy, and internally there is a voice spewing thoughts of resistance, judgment, self-doubt, and irritation. What have you gotten yourself into? The dessert table at the holiday party is *your* thing . . . and now Jackie has ruined some of your fun. Maybe you'll just slip in some butter and not tell her.

We'll leave that story for now. Do you see how an inner voice began to narrate negative thoughts in your mind based on what was happening and the stories in your vegan file?

We want to name these sour thoughts, similar to how we personified the amygdala as AMY. We call this other heavy-impact player, another invisible force, the *Inner Narrator*.

YOUR INNER NARRATOR UNDER PRESSURE

It's common for many people to experience some form of inner speech.[4] Research shows that some people hear an internal voice that expresses thoughts and opinions. Some people don't "hear" a voice, per se, but rather "just have thoughts." Either way, most human minds are chattering with an ongoing "monologue" of thoughts.

Can you hear your thoughts? Is there a voice? Do you feel it's separate from "you?" Do you engage in an internal "dialogue," with your own voice? Sometimes do you dialogue, fight, or have conversations with other internal voices[5] that represent people in the external world?

Have you ever replayed an argument in your mind, looping it over and over? Maybe each time the voices becoming louder and the words harsher, until you lose recollection of what actually happened because the fight is so amplified in your mind, and all of a sudden you can't stand that person and have no desire to bridge the gap with them, only to realize, later, that in reality your Inner Narrator may have overreacted, creating a mountain out of a molehill?

Let's go back to Francisco. In his case, he admitted that he struggles to like Julius. In his mind, he probably hears "Julius's" voice—poking and prodding about the ½ cent tax. But, that's not actually Julius's real voice or thoughts, right? It's a representation of what Francisco's Inner Narrator thinks Julius would say—and it's tainted by Francisco's emotional needs to be understood, accepted, and valued.

It could get dicey for Francisco if he is unaware of his thinking and believes that his Inner Narrator is representing Julius's *real* voice. Over time, if Francisco becomes more and more irritated with Julius, then that could drive a further wedge between them—even though nothing more happened between them in real life. Francisco's Inner Narrator could turn sour and hijack all of his wonderful tools to be in a working relationship with Julius. For instance, Francisco's ego could possibly turn defensive, wanting to protect his way of doing things and start to think: *Screw that guy! I don't need him to be part of what I'm doing anyway. Julius is a jerk, his opinions don't matter cause he doesn't know what he's talking about, and my team doesn't need that energy.*

Your mind and Inner Narrator manufacture a wide spectrum of thoughts and stories throughout the day, which are often born out of your emotions. Nobody is immune. And it's important to acknowledge that your thoughts and stories are not always negative or false. The key is to have awareness about when your Inner Narrator turns sour, judgmental, and uber-critical. And that's usually when your emotional needs aren't being met. When you feel misunderstood, disliked, rejected, underappreciated, or devalued. Or when you feel challenged by the unfamiliar . . . like Jackie asking you to make vegan cupcakes.

▶ The Big Aha! ◀

When you're challenged with the unfamiliar, under pressure, and your emotional needs aren't being met, your mind fires up a soured Inner Narrator that distracts you from having clarity about the truth of the situation.

Here's another simple example. Perhaps part of your job is to manage social media for a small local boutique. Between working the register, you work diligently and carefully to promote and reflect a compelling image about the products and store. Your boss comes in and claims you are being "lazy" by not posting enough. Your Inner Narrator likely trash talks your boss as she makes this accusation about your performance . . . when in fact, you spend one to two hours every other day responding to the public's comments in the threads . . . which she never bothers to read. Therefore, she doesn't see your contributions and isn't valuing your efforts. It's an easy misunderstanding to clean up: show your boss how well you're responding to and handling comments in the threads. Don't create a bunch of drama because your Inner Narrator has gone sour. That's useless and disconnects you from maintaining open communication with your boss.

Often therapists say, "Don't believe everything you think or feel."[6] Take heed of that warning because when AMY and the Inner Narrator are hijacking you with overwhelmingly negative thoughts, it can provoke unnecessary shame, anxiety, and worry.

Here is another way to look at it. Let's say that you found Becky, your colleague, furiously scrubbing out the office microwave one afternoon. You've never cleaned the microwave before and assumed the janitorial staff took care of it at night. You remember a stupid childhood joke that your mom taught you about microwaves and blurt it out. "Becky! What happened when the tin foil and leftovers went on a date in the microwave? They shared an explosive meal." You chuckle, despite the fact that once you've uttered the joke out loud you realize it isn't that funny. It was how your mom taught you to not place metal in the microwave. Becky stops scrubbing, turns, and before she says anything, you catch a look on her face that you interpret as irritated. You fumble and say, "Oh, sorry. I didn't make a mess in the microwave. Just trying to make you laugh, sorry." She shakes her head and returns to the microwave. None of it landed well and now you feel awkward.

Later, you're in a meeting with Becky and it seems like she won't even look at you. Your worry turns to panic because in the past you've done nothing but fumble with Becky. At every turn, you tend to look like an idiot in front her. To that end, your Inner Narrator provides the evidence for you to believe that you're a buffoon when it comes to her. This voice interrupts the rest of your workday with stories about how annoying Becky must find you. At the end of the day, you walk by her office and bravely decide to pop your head in and explain that "this microwave thing is a big misunderstanding." Becky looks confused and says, "What are you talking about?" You explain how your mom taught you this lame joke as a kid, and she says, "Oh that? I struggle to hear in my left ear and couldn't really hear what you were saying with my head in the microwave. I left my soup in too long and it bubbled over. I was just annoyed at myself."

What a misunderstanding! That's the power of when a story is fabricated in your mind.

In this case, the Inner Narrator provided you with a series of stories from a file in your limbic system called "Becky." They pulled out only the stories where you were awkward with her. The story is: *You're an idiot in front of Becky.* This makes you nervous around her, unable to communicate and collaborate. Also, notice how in this instance, the Inner Narrator didn't turn negative toward Becky—blaming her for the awkwardness. Instead, the Inner Narrator turned on you—blaming you for being a fumbling idiot.

In these moments of pressure, it's important to have the awareness to understand that your story about Becky is not about Becky—it's about you. Going into the office to approach Becky was brave—and that's what it takes to disrupt an Inner Narrator.

Francisco doesn't even allow his Inner Narrator to go there. He acknowledges that he has the same old story in his mind about Julius and therefore refuses to give into negative beliefs about Julius. By engaging in psychological distance, Francisco doesn't allow the file in his mind destroy the relationship that they do have, even if it's not a pleasant one.

Moment by moment, you have a choice about how you engage with someone where there is a gap—even when AMY hijacks you and your Inner Narrator is spewing negative thoughts.

We want to give you a way to disrupt the Inner Narrator when it manufactures damaging stories. Perhaps, like Francisco, you will disrupt your soured Inner Narrator by reflecting back to yourself in the third person to gain a sense of perspective. If this feels silly, try naming your Inner Narrator with a different name than your own. Similar to how we personified AMY, try creating more psychological distance between you and the soured thoughts in your mind with a clever or laughable name to remind you that your negative inner thoughts do not define you. If you choose to try this, then maybe Mr. Grumpy or Ms. Sassafrass will do the job.

Another way to dramatically disrupt a soured inner voice is to shift how you think about stories, others, and yourself through a metaphorical kaleidoscope.

THE POWER OF KALEIDOSCOPES

In your childhood, did you ever play with a kaleidoscope? Become sucked into the shape-shifting beauty of a world reconfiguring itself through its lens?

A kaleidoscope is an oblong tube of loose jewels and internal mirrors. The jewels shift when you twist one end of the tube slightly one way or the other. On the other end is a small peephole to view inside. When the jewels move, they tumble into a new arrangement, refracting off the internal mirror and incoming light to create different fractal patterns. You never see the same fractal pattern twice, as the jewels never move or shift in the exact same way.

We love this metaphor to describe how your mind is no different.

Your mind is the container itself. The jewels inside are pressure, society, ego, culture, education, memories, DNA, family of origin, joy, trauma, emotions, and many other variables in your life. The pattern that those jewels make reflects the story that you inhabit and view as truth. When you shift your kaleidoscope, new patterns appear and you evaluate them differently.

This is beyond the art of "reframing." A reframe approach is like taking a snapshot of a static picture from different angles. The kaleidoscope effect is a redesign of the entire picture, and not just a redesign of one frame or angle, but an entirely new picture with every single shift of the kaleidoscope. This is how you begin to shift your thinking and embrace a new perspective.

So, when your Inner Narrator speaks to you about "how it really is," beware and be cautious. Take it with a grain of salt. Shift your kaleidoscope and focus on different jewels to reveal

new patterns—new ways of seeing the story or situation, especially the people you're struggling to connect, communicate, and
collaborate with.

Remember, to bridge the gap, we have to move *closer* to people, not farther away in our discomfort. That likely means that we
need to find a way to see them in a new light. How will you find
ways to understand, like, and value them when there is a gap? The
kaleidoscope effect helps.

For instance, Francisco doesn't like how Julius shows up to
fight for his perspective on the sales tax measure. Francisco knows
that if he wants to have a unified front, he needs the support of
Julius and his customers. He acknowledges that there are sub-
stantial gaps between them—they don't share the same culture,
language, generation, or approach to life. Julius threatens and
yells to get people's attention. Francisco uses small talk, charm,
and a smile to gain influence. Francisco, in his psychological flexibility and distancing, is able to hush his soured Inner Narrator
and focus on common ground—both men want a thriving business community and support the residents in the neighborhood.

Francisco decides to take Julius to coffee. They make awkward
small talk, and then Francisco boldy, but warmly, asks, "What do
you really want in this fight, and if you don't win the fight, what is
at stake for your business and clients?" Then he is quiet.

He listens as Julius spills language that is sometimes still
mean, angry, and vindictive. During Julius's talking, it's clear
that he doesn't truly trust or respect Francisco and is giving him a
piece of his mind. Francisco breathes. He doesn't react, not when
AMY or his Inner Narrator are pushing him to. Eventually, Julius
calms down and is quieter.

Francisco carefully relays back to Julius the points where
they share a common goal . . . and surprisingly one of them has
to do with repaving the parking lots in front of Julius's business.
Francisco shared with us that he never knew the blacktop was a
big deal to Julius. Francisco has found a common anchor and is
able to move Julius to bigger issues and gain some of his support.

Let's go back to Jackie the vegan. Could you, the amazing
sugary sweet baker that you are, twist your kaleidoscope to see
Jackie's good intentions? She is trying to belong to the office

holiday party. She is trying to honor you as the amazing dessert baker in the office. She isn't trying to make you feel bad for loving butter. Could you embrace that she is stretching your culinary skills—and that you might even find out that vegan cupcakes taste delicious?

This is real work of becoming a better communicator and relationship builder. It's the real work of bridging the gap.

There is no zipper or escape hatch—we are in our human suits forever. Pressure, AMY, a soured Inner Narrator, and being challenged are all here to stay. Becoming self-aware never comes without discomfort. But pull out your kaleidoscope and try to see something beautiful by breaking up your patterned thinking.

New stories can bloom. You can write a new story. You can view your lived experiences in a new light. The beauty of it all is that you really do have the power to become self-aware about how you behave and show up, what you think and say.

REFLECTION QUESTIONS

- What patterns do you see in your thinking?
- What is the dialogue, loop, or monologue of your Inner Narrator when under pressure?
- What do you need to apply a kaleidoscope effect to in your professional (or personal) life right now? How might you view things differently to show up better?

ACTION ITEM
The Choice: Kaleidoscope over Inner Narrator

Identify a story that you consistently tell over and over again, to others and/or to yourself. In this story, try to gain some psychological distance and see yourself as a character. In this distancing, you are only able to see yourself as an actor on stage, unable to wholly feel the interior world and motives. You can only see your actions and uttered words. What patterns emerge when you view other repetitive stories of yours with psychological distance? Does a narrative emerge that uncovers how you position yourself in relation to others?

Consider copying Francisco's Monday morning ritual for one full month. For fifteen minutes at the start of your work week, you'll go to a private place (your car, office, bathroom) and talk OUT LOUD to yourself as if you were a character that you read about in a book—even if it feels silly, stupid, or immature. You will comment upon what you did, felt, said, thought, and more. Make notes to see if you can identify patterns in how you think, the quality of your thoughts, and what your stories have in common. Consider naming your soured Inner Narrator something clever or laughable to remind you that your negative inner thoughts do not define you.

JOIN THE CONVERSATION AND INTERACT ONLINE

#shiftyourkaleidoscope

RELATIONSHIP DYNAMICS
The Drama Triangle or the Circle of Choice

So far, you've learned about the impact of AMY and the Inner Narrator on how you show up to connect, communicate, and collaborate. In this chapter, we introduce you to the last impact player that you need to be aware of—and disrupt—to improve your relationships and communication. It's a toxic relationship dynamic in which many people unconsciously become stuck.

Michael grabs his cup of coffee and walks to the conference room for a meeting where he is going to present his ideas for the fall clothing line. Usually this is his favorite time of season: Reveal Day. A meeting where the lead designers unveil their creative work and concepts to the full team. Michael considers himself a team player. In particular, he delights in collaborating about new fabrics, exploring what's *hot* and *stylish* in textures and colors, and figuring out with the team how it all comes together for their customers in a collection.

But all that seems to be in the rearview mirror.

Michael can admit that he feels differently about Reveal Day now . . . and knows what's about to come his way. When he presents, everyone is going to smile, nod, and yet again ignore his valuable contributions. With over thirty years' experience in a top men's designer clothing brand, he is one of the oldest lead designers on staff, but due to that experience he knows what it takes to accomplish a good fall collection—and it's pretty straightforward. Michael believes that men's fashion doesn't change that much and neither do men. But no one seems that interested in his wisdom or sense of timeless tradition and classics or really anything he has to contribute.

Walking to the door of the conference room, he hears them inside: his colleagues' passion and excitement for Reveal Day. There is laughter, nervousness, and an excitable energy. As he enters, he remembers those feelings, too. But now they—and him—are invisible. Unseen ghosts of the past, simply thrown out and discarded because of his age.

He takes his place at the table and sits in the chair that has held and swiveled him for years. He lays down his portfolio with printouts of his digital "look book" in front of him and paws through them when Stephanie, a youthful designer known for producing fun, special-occasion bow ties, walks over and says hi. Michael remains seated and can barely muster any chitchat. He continues to flip through his concepts as she tries to engage him about what he did over the weekend, but he's hijacked by the continuous, nagging feeling that he's outdated.

Then Trent arrives.

"Hi Michael! I'm eager to see what you have for us today." He smiles and turns to Stephanie, "And you're just the person I'm looking for—can I get your thoughts, Steph, about a bow tie idea that I'm tinkering with?"

Michael's negative feelings amplify with Trent's presence. Instead of joining their conversation, Michael continues to stay seated and scoots his chair closer to the table, allowing the two millennials to stand at his back. He overhears how Trent thinks that bow ties have finally crossed over as an everyday staple in the dressers of many urban professional men who are choosing to wear them to work over traditional ties.

"There could be a huge market here—want to partner on it with me?" Trent asks Stephanie, which of course, Michael overhears. Stephanie responds by confirming the trends that she's seeing emerge on Instagram and Tik Tok and says, "Hell, yeah!" to Trent.

Everything about this conversation irks Michael. His Inner Narrator fires off bombs like:

> That golden child, Trent, of course, will nail it today. And there goes Stephanie like everyone else, always oohing and aahing over him and his "original" ideas . . . when all he really does is just recycle s@%t and calls it something new. Yeah, we'll see how long the bow tie trend lasts . . . ha! Men don't know how to tie them on their way out the door in the morning and the prefabricated ones look cheap. What idiots . . . But what do I know, Trent? Definitely don't ask to partner with me, the one who actually invented the best bow tie that ever sold in this company at one point.

When Trent came into the business, Michael initially liked him. But now, he is struggling to value him.

Trent is ten years into his career. Hired to be a fresh voice in men's fashion and to bring a new generational lens, Trent is smart and sharp. He's a great designer with creative ideas around product development, but more importantly, Trent can strategically parlay those into new distribution channels for the company. His innovative approaches have yielded a new set of customers to the business, which is struggling to grow beyond its stale name and branding. Embracing social media advertising, influencers, and clickfunnel marketing, Trent has expanded the company's reach, becoming the *go-to guy* for the CEO and the COO.

It's easy to see that Trent is embraced by all while Michael feels marginalized, disregarded. The dynamics are palpable.

Today, on his beloved Reveal Day, Michael can hardly stand it anymore. His pride is making him see green. He has not spoken directly to Trent in the past few weeks. He's decided—or at least his Inner Narrator has—that Trent isn't worth his energy. And Kayla, the assistant of the CEO, agrees. Michael feels lucky to have her on on his side, and after having worked closely with her for more than twenty years, he believes that Kayla is extremely aware about what is going on—a new hotshot distracting them from what real men actually want to buy.

In lieu of making small talk with the other designers before Reveal Day begins, Michael pulls out his phone and texts Kayla: "Here we go again 🙄!"

Kayla responds: "He is a flash in the pan . . . you have experience so stop worrying and I'll talk up your ideas for you on my next 1-1 w/ the boss 😀!"

Michael smirks; he is grateful that Kayla sees it as clearly as he does and is fighting for him. Whenever he feels unsupported or rejected by the group (or management), Kayla is always there to receive his complaints and whining, and so Michael always walks away feeling validated and encouraged.

Michael texts back: "You're my rock 😇 Thx!"

Of course, generational issues in the workplace are common—and too easy to dismiss as just a difference of age. While Michael's situation is tied to the years that span between him and Trent, Michael is playing into a relationship dynamic that is deeper than simply being jealous of the hotshot on the team. Michael has slid into something called the Drama Triangle.

THE DRAMA TRIANGLE

The Drama Triangle, developed by Dr. Stephen Karpman, is a relationship paradigm/dynamic that explains a set of behavioral roles that we consciously or unconsciously play out with people.[1] The roles that we inhabit in the Drama Triangle create relationship dynamics that often pit people against one another. Essentially, the Drama Triangle widens the gap and disintegrates the quality communication and collaboration you and others can experience. Unfortunately, this paradigm and the dynamics it creates between people surrounds us everywhere, not only at work. We see it in our marriages, in our interactions with our children, in how our friends talk about their lives, and in nearly every story we consume. It appears in sitcoms, dramas, bestselling books, fairy tales, Disney classics, and blockbusters that we watched and read in our formative years. The plots all follow the same basic outline:

1. Someone (or some outside force) is coordinating conflict and drama to gain a form of power, sometimes resulting in harm and trauma: *Darth Vader and the Empire.*

2. Someone is caught in their web, helpless and stuck, in need of rescuing: *The Rebels*.
3. Someone heeds the call and becomes the savior: *Luke Skywalker*.

The Drama Triangle occurs the most when someone's fundamental emotional needs are at stake. Michael feels devalued and therefore he slides into the Drama Triangle to try and make sense of his strong emotions. In his case, the Drama Triangle offers his soured Inner Narrator a reliable story about who should pay for making him feel a certain way, losing credibility with his peers as a designer, and struggling to keep up with new fashion trends and marketing streams.

You probably learned and mastered this relationship dynamic unconsciously in your childhood. Many of you unconsciously adopted various behavioral roles at an early age and began a neural-wiring process that, over time, told you how to show up and communicate in places where conflict is brewing or occurring. Because you cannot zip off your human suit, it is guaranteed that you will be sucked into the Drama Triangle at work and beyond. The Drama Triangle dynamic consists of three key roles:

- *Persecutor: "It's all your fault!"* The persecutor (sometimes called the villain) can be a person, set of people, or a situation that uses blame and criticism to control, manipulate, and/or gain power. The persecutor subconsciously scans environments to interact with victims.
- *Victim: "Poor me!"* The victim sees life as happening to them and often feels stuck and unable to change their circumstance. They often feel powerless to stand up for themselves and tend to be super sensitive. Victims subconsciously look to blame persecutors and seek out rescuers to solve their problems for them.
- *Rescuer: "Let me help you!"* The classic hero, the rescuer behaves as an enabler who feels it is their job to the rescue those who can't help themselves. Rescuers find value in being needed by others and can be seen as the savior. They work hard to save people at the expense of their own health and

tend to not allow others to figure it out. While playing this
role at work or home may seem altruistic, it is dysfunctional
as it creates dependency with the victim.

Exhibit 4.1 shows what the Drama Triangle looks like.

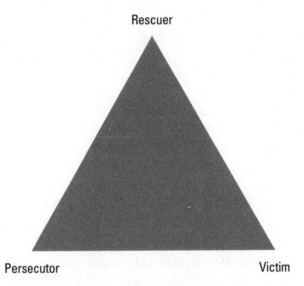

EXHIBIT 4.1 The Drama Triangle

These are typically the three unconscious roles that people
inhabit when:

- They are struggling to understand, like, or respect someone
  that threatens their way of thinking, being, or doing things.
- They are under pressure and hijacked by AMY.
- Their emotional needs aren't being met.
- Their Inner Narrator goes sour and starts feeding unhelpful
  stories.
- Conflict is brewing, emotions are high, and something
  valuable is at stake.

The roles are not actual people, nor are they fixed. Most people bounce between playing the three roles of *victim, persecutor,*
and *rescuer.* Sometimes the rescuer and the victim are the same

person. Sometimes the persecutor and the rescuer are the same person. Sometimes the victim and the persecutor are the same person. Sometimes we play all three and engage in self-punishment, self-sabotage, self-victimization, and self-saving.

Finally, the Drama Triangle can happen entirely in someone's head, or it can play out in real life, or some combination of the two. Either way, this toxic relationship paradigm is present and damaging to connection, communication, and collaboration. It is easy to slide into the Drama Triangle or be pulled into it by someone else.

In Michael's case, he slid into the Drama Triangle dynamic with full force. At first glance, it's easy to assign the roles based on Michael's perspective: Michael is the victim, Trent is the persecutor, and Kayla is the savior.

However, Trent didn't even sign up to play this role. Michael slid him into the paradigm to make sense of his own frustration, disappointment, and psychological inflexibility. Trent doesn't even know that he's been slid into the Drama Triangle. However, he can sense that Michael is upset with him and that's why he doesn't ask Michael to collaborate on the bow ties and potential market. Kayla doesn't know she's been slid into the Drama Triangle. She is just trying to support her friend who is annoyed with the young guy. However, for Michael, Trent and Kayla are key players in the tension he feels about Reveal Day.

To that end, Michael is both the persecutor (of Trent) and the victim (of Trent), saved by Kayla who strokes his ego when he's feeling insecure about his designs for Reveal Day, being older than most of the designers, and in comparison to Trent.

Unfortunately, the Drama Triangle is a story that Michael can live inside for a long time . . . and to his own personal and professional detriment. And it's a story that many of us slide into without even acknowledging being caught in its trap.

Do you work with someone who triangulates like this? Do you find yourself listening to someone at work whose typical story pattern is:

- *Victim:* They're constantly put upon and can't keep up. Woe is me. Nobody appreciates how hard they work. The powers that be are out to get them with rules, policies, procedures or the lack thereof. Something is never right. There is always something bad that has happened or is about to happen around the corner.

- *Persecutor:* They're constantly blaming, shaming, and criticizing other people's work and output. This may show up as sarcasm, gossip, complaining, or plain old bullying. Things are rarely, if ever, their fault.
- *Rescuer:* They're constantly working on something only they can do. As the savior, they are the only one who *actually does things right.* They struggle to collaborate, often because they claim people are helpless or too busy to do their parts well or on time. This may show up as being the martyr, the grand all-knower, the one with the history and knowledge and "how-to."

These roles that people play drive unnecessary drama and aren't productive for any work environment. Drama and excessive pressure affect the brain and lead to poor decision-making, stress, disengaged employees, and increased sick leave. Therefore, the Drama Triangle paradigm is extremely costly from an HR and financial standpoint. The Drama Triangle causes enormous disruption in productivity, efficiency, team morale, and profitability when organizations allow—or promote—this type of triangulation or toxic paradigm where people are pitted against one another.

Did we just say *promote?*

Yep.

We have worked inside several enterprises where the Drama Triangle or some form of it is not only allowed but encouraged. Often, the leader is unaware of the resultant negative dynamics of the Drama Triangle and slides into it as a strategy to move people to action by creating a sense of "healthy competition." They use the power of consequence—the losing of something valuable. Or perhaps they use the allure of a reward to move people to action. For instance, one of our clients had a "leader and loser" board displayed at work for a sales competition. The reward was a $1,000 plane voucher, and the team was encouraged to do anything it took to accomplish their goals. The phrase they threw around was "steal for a deal." It gave permission for staff to compete for inbound leads to cross the finish line first. While initially intended as good old-fashioned fun, it quickly became a source of gaming and shaming. The drama was egged on within text strands and at the daily stand-up meeting. The team slid into the Drama Triangle and played a vicious game. The cost was an enormous loss of trust for everybody involved.

While playful competition and awards are okay in the workplace, engaging in this dynamic as a main strategy to motivate people to success is a poor choice. In the long-term, pitting people against each other engages the brain in unhealthy patterning that doesn't allow people to collaborate or communicate when times are stressful or sticky.

The Drama Triangle paradigm and similar relationship-based structures prevent people from working together, innovating, and being focused on accomplishing important, shared goals that require everyone's diverse expertise, talents, and ideas mingling together. For example, the allowance of gossip and indirect communication inside an organization is insidious. When there is a culture where this is allowed, people will slide right into the Drama Triangle, destroying trust, collaboration, and respect. This must be squashed, quickly and firmly, if your goal is to bridge the gap.

So, aware of it or not, when people are in a relationship dynamic that mimics the structure of the Drama Triangle, it causes damage at multiple levels, creating that toxic work environment that every manager fears. Being able to identify the Drama Triangle and the poor behaviors that exist inside it—yours and/ or another's—is one of the most powerful tools you can use to see how breakdowns happen. This is where you can really become bridge-builders in your relationships at work—by stepping out of the Drama Triangle and disrupting the dynamics by refusing to play one of its behavioral roles.

Warning—it's not easy! Drama Triangles are easy to slide into. Let's look at how quickly we can get sucked into drama.

Monday 8:15 A.M.: Conference Room

Irritated Tim: "Seriously, Gina? Of all days to be late. We have a tight deadline." (Persecutor.)

Late Gina: "I'm sooooo sorry! It wasn't my fault—there must have been a car accident or something on the freeway. I'm only fifteen minutes late. I would have been here in plenty of time if not for that!" (Victim of traffic.)

Hijacked Tim: "But I guess you still had time to grab a Starbucks for yourself on the way in?" (Persecutor.)

Coworkers Matt and Valerie: "To be fair, the traffic was awful this morning. Look, Valerie, don't be upset—we can help all pitch in and get it done." (Rescuers.)

Disgruntled Tim: "That's not the point—we all have responsibilities, and I don't like being put into a tight timeline like this. It reflects poorly on me." (Shifts to Victim.)

Hijacked Gina: "Look, I said sorry. So, I have coffee—kill me. Let's just get to work and get it done and stop wasting time. And by the way, what we turn in reflects on all of us, not just you." (Shifts to persecutor.)

Coworkers Matt and Valerie: "Calm down everyone, we worked on the documents last night—let's give them a final look before the presentation." (Rescuers.)

That thirty second interaction slid this group of hard-working individuals into a dynamic that unfortunately set the tone for the presentation. That energy carried into their presentation.

So, how will you exit the Drama Triangle when these situations appear and threaten your ability to connect, communicate, and collaborate well?

FROM THE DRAMA TRIANGLE TO THE CIRCLE OF CHOICE

It's likely that you slide into playing a default role when you struggle to understand, like, or respect someone at work or beyond. When you slide into that default role, you open the Drama Triangle, creating a door for unnecessary conflict, irritation, and more, to enter. When you're in a triangle story you will feel poked, prodded, manipulated, and tense.

We're not going to lie, many people are addicted to the Drama Triangle story because it's embedded in our culture, and it places us on a rollercoaster ride of emotions, distractions, and cheap thrills. The Drama Triangle is anything but boring. It provides you with adrenaline—and most people love the rush.

But don't take the bait. Don't bite when the fishing line is dropped in the conflict pool and your favorite way to behave is dangled in front of your nose.

It's all too easy to slide into old behaviors and roles, especially when you're hijacked by AMY and the soured Inner Narrators manufacturing stories in your head. It's so natural, you don't even notice you've slid into a Drama Triangle. The key is to recognize that the role you are playing—or have been placed in, like Trent— isn't real. It does not have to define you. You have a choice to either engage with the sharp dynamics of a triangle or step out and create different outcomes.

While triangles poke and prod you with their sharp edges and hard roles, we use the image of a circle to explain an opposite paradigm that is available to you to enter. In the Circle of Choice (shown in Exhibit 4.2), you access personal responsibility, self-awareness, and psychological flexibility. In the Circle of Choice, you choose to psychologically distance yourself from your feelings and agenda to be right and/or to win. You pull out a kaleidoscope to see things shift and fall into new ways. By doing so, you are not allowing AMY to spew negativity, and this is how you reshape and wire your brain.

The Circle of Choice represents infinite flow of energy, choices, and opportunities. Indeed, it is the antithesis of the triangle. The Circle of Choice is what we use to call people into being composed, not reactive. The Circle of Choice represents the following empowering choices we can make when struggling in the Drama Triangle:

* ***You are the author of your reality.*** You have a choice about how you engage with your stories. You can evaluate how you have shown up in the past and reflect on when your relationships and communication failed and when it thrived. You can create a story—a hopeful one that you want to

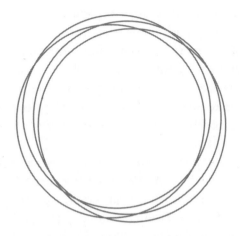

EXHIBIT 4.2 The Circle of Choice

happen in this present moment. Whatever comes your way, you can always feel, think, and interpret information differently if you practice psychological flexibility. You always have choice in how you show up with people at work and beyond.

- **You are response-able.** You were born with a prefrontal cortex that is gifted with metacognition, the ability to think about thinking and make different decisions. The lion doesn't evaluate her behavior when she pounces on the gazelle. You are not a reactive lion. You are (now) aware of AMY, a soured Inner Narrator, and the Drama Triangle. You can disrupt your reactions when hijacked (we'll provide you with proven, reliable strategies in the next chapter). You can extract yourself from toxic relationship dynamics by refusing to play one of the three roles. You can choose to move closer and be curious with the person you struggle to understand, like, or respect. You can build a better relationship.

- **You can step up and bridge the gap.** Yes—the choice is yours. You don't have to wait for permission or for the boss to tell you to do it. You can become a person who thinks clearly and productively, who uses curiosity as a lens to understand that which may make you feel threatened (we'll teach you how in Chapter 6). You can hush your Inner Narrator when it finds fraudulent evidence that keeps you captive in a harsh Drama Triangle. You can exercise conscious psychological flexibility and distancing to see how your stories unfold when you're with someone. You can seek to understand the person in front of you, and honor their fundamental emotional needs. Even when it's tough. You can honor the fact that they, too, are worthy of being seen as valuable.

Stop playing these roles and step out of the triangle and choose the circle. Your brain, mind, and spirit will thank you for ridding them of unnecessary drama. So will your colleagues, your boss, your family, and more.

MOVING TO THE CIRCLE AND GETTING BACK TO WORK

There really is only one solution: have acute awareness and take personal responsibility to get yourself out of the triangle and into the circle, where productive communication and collaboration lives.

➤ The Big Aha! ◀

Is the default role that I am inhabiting and playing inside the Drama Triangle working for me? Is my perspective causing suffering? Is it making me stuck in a relationship that I want to escape? Is the way I play any of these roles widening the gap that I need to close? And if so . . . is it time to change how I show up and engage?

If you find yourself sliding into a **victim** role, ask yourself:

* What is the story that I am telling myself right now? Am I really powerless or stuck? Do I really need others to step up?
* What's something I can do, right now, that will allow me to feel empowered? Write it down, make a plan, and act on it.

- How am I showing up at work? Am I always apologizing? Am I always complaining about what's out of my control? Time to reflect on those patterns.
- Am I being honest about the role I've played in the relationship and/or communication breakdown? What can I do differently?

If you find yourself sliding into a **persecutor** role, ask yourself:

- How do I want to show up that is supportive and engaging, not belittling and marginalizing?
- How am I being experienced? Am I harsh? Am I sarcastic? Am I dominating?
- Am I looking to be seen or to support and collaborate?
- Am I actually here to listen and be curious about others?
- Can I use my assertiveness instead to support others in their growth and development?

If you find yourself sliding into a **rescuer** role, ask yourself:

- What is driving my need to play a savior in this situation?
- How can I empower this individual or team instead of doing it for them?
- How can I collaborate and help others to grow instead of taking on the tasks myself?
- How can I stop giving answers and start posing questions to others to help them figure out how to do things?

Our story of Michael and Trent doesn't end well. There was no bridging the gap because, in the end, Michael refused to acknowledge any wrongdoing. He dug in his corner. He gave a pathetic, limp sorry. He wasn't even a shade curious about what might be happening. He was always the victim of what he called "generational politics." Michael continued, meeting after meeting, to discredit Trent. He became louder and louder with his sarcasm, criticisms, and accusations. Kayla stopped coming to his side as a rescuer when he pressured her to say negative things about Trent in front of their boss. The gap became a canyon. Then he tried to pull more people like Kayla into his triangle and lost even more credibility among the staff. Along the way, Michael continued to destroy his reputation. Longtime colleagues lost respect for Michael . . . they didn't understand "what happened." They said, *He used to be a nice guy—one of the best!* Then one day Michael totally went off, inappropriately, hurling accusations against Trent. The CEO decided to fire him.

Michael could have easily stood up when Stephanie came over and talked bow ties. He could have even stayed when Trent arrived to talk about bow ties and the new market potential. Instead, he stewed at the conference table, flipping through his design book, looking at all the fashion that wouldn't make it to the stores because he defaulted into a role that served his pride. He met his demise in the Drama Triangle.

REFLECTION QUESTIONS

- What drama triangle role do you notice yourself sliding into most frequently?
- Where do you identify the drama triangle playing out at work? At home? In your community?
- How might you say no to participating in a drama triangle when someone "invites" you in with them?

ACTION ITEM

The Choice: Circle of Choice over Drama Triangle

Identify your default role in the Drama Triangle. Then spend a few days watching Drama Triangles play out. If you're in one, choose intentionally how you will engage from the Circle of Choice and not take the bait from the triangle. If you meet with someone who pulls, slides, or drags you into the Drama Triangle, prepare in advance how you'll show up.

JOIN THE CONVERSATION AND INTERACT ONLINE

#choosethecircleofchoice

SHOW UP CLEAN
Disrupt the Hijack and Invisible Forces
even more

I n the last three chapters, you learned how three *invisible forces*—
AMY, a soured Inner Narrator, and the Drama Triangle—can
easily hijack you from being a good communicator, especially in
relationships where you experience a gap.

And let's be honest . . . you may have read those last three
chapters and thought: *But I'm not the one with the problem—the
other person is hijacked by AMY, their Inner Narrator, and has
placed me in their Drama Triangle. I am doing my best.*

You are.

And they are doing the best they can, too.

If you find yourself being suspicious of that last sentence,
then we'd like to expand on it: *At any given moment, we must
acknowledge that the majority of people are doing the best that
they can with the skills that they can access when under the pressure they're experiencing.* We all react and respond differently to
the constant pressure that comes with living inside a human suit.

When these invisible forces hijack people who are already
struggling in the finger trap, their tendency is to *pull further* away
and become stuck even more. If you want to be released from the
finger trap, then someone in the relationship must move closer and
push toward the other(s) to bridge the gap.

And because you're reading this book, that's *you.*

We need *you* to be the person who shows up with the tool-box that will begin constructing the bridge . . . because you can't force, cajole, convince, or bait the other person to change. You likely can't ignore or make them disappear. These strategies might make you feel like you've taken care of the "problem," but they don't release you from the finger trap.

The gap you need to close likely stems from fundamental emotional needs not being met on either side. We showed this before (in Chapter 2), but here it is again, as Exhibit 5.1.

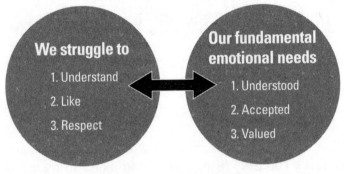

EXHIBIT 5.1 The Gap to Bridge

Of course, we've witnessed people argue against this model. They speak with certainty that they have no issues with someone, but then offer a vague response about how another's lack of skill and/or immaturity is the real gap. Have you heard—or said—statements like the following?

- "I have no problem with Bob; it's just that he messes up projects more than he helps. I often have to clean up his work, on top of my own. He needs to learn to multitask better and make a proper spreadsheet. Then I would have no issue with working with him." (Note: This speaker struggles to value Bob's contributions at work.)
- "Sheila is a wonderful woman; she just needs ten more years of management experience before becoming our leader." (Note: This speaker struggles to respect Sheila and see what she does bring as a leader.)

- "Millennials want everything right now. They are an entitled generation that hasn't paid their dues like we have. Sara will need to wait before we ever consider her for that promotion." (Note: This speaker struggles to understand an entire generation and is punishing Sara for her age and ambition.)
- "OK, Betty, show me again how to create a coordinated influencer campaign across five social media platforms using a data-driven algorithm that allows us to respond in real time to people's feeds. Oh, that's right. Boomers don't know how." (Note: This speaker struggles to like an entire generation and speaks with sarcasm that damages relationships.)

Do you hear judgments and assumptions in each of those statements?

Generational, cultural, and skill gaps exists. And sometimes they aren't just gaps between people, they are entire canyons to cross.

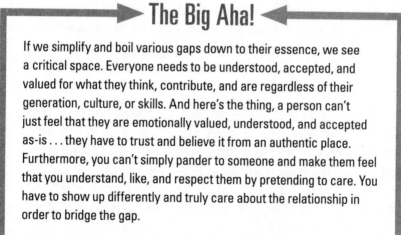

The Big Aha!

If we simplify and boil various gaps down to their essence, we see a critical space. Everyone needs to be understood, accepted, and valued for what they think, contribute, and are regardless of their generation, culture, or skills. And here's the thing, a person can't just feel that they are emotionally valued, understood, and accepted as-is . . . they have to trust and believe it from an authentic place. Furthermore, you can't simply pander to someone and make them feel that you understand, like, and respect them by pretending to care. You have to show up differently and truly care about the relationship in order to bridge the gap.

You *can* bridge the gap in meaningful, authentic ways that meet crucial emotional needs. You *can* address honest and critical feedback with people who don't share the same value system, perspectives, backgrounds, or diversity of thought. Now that you're aware of, and understand, the power of the three invisible forces, we will teach you how throughout the rest of the book.

Your first step in communicating better, in any relationship, is to show up *clean and curious*. Can you? (The answer is "yes"!)

YOUR FIRST GAP TO BRIDGE: THE SPACE BETWEEN READINESS AND RESISTANCE

Are you ready to:

* Move closer to someone who gets under your skin?
* Take personal responsibility for all of your thoughts, behaviors, and actions?
* Be curious about what you *don't know that you don't know* about a person that you're struggling to understand, like, or respect?
* Approach someone who doesn't understand, accept, or value you?
* Hear something new—even if it is critical feedback about how you communicate and collaborate?
* Try new, possibly uncomfortable, things to disrupt your default, habitually wired reactions?
* Have that crucial or fraught conversation?
* Change how you show up and engage?

If you answered "yes"—terrific! It's likely, however, that you answered "maybe," or "I don't know," or with a flat-out "no." That's okay. One of our beliefs is that people live on a spectrum somewhere between readiness and resistance.

When people experience *resistance,* they grapple with obstacles—real or perceived, external or internal—and that blocks them from changing behaviors.

When people experience *readiness,* they feel a desire to move toward whatever they have to do to change core behaviors.

Your job is to close the gap between readiness and resistance for yourself and for those you desire to build more meaningful relationships with.

Nearly all humans struggle with behavioral change because our biology views change as a threat. This is called "Immunity to Change" theory.[1] Your biology has built an "immune system" over time to protect and defend how you (your ego, culture, mindset, knowledge, personality, and more) operate in the world. No matter how desperate you are to improve, your brain and mind work against your desires and attempts to build better, healthier habits.

This plays out every year during our New Years' resolutions—we create an exciting goal, feel readiness, launch, and then are met with various forms of resistance. We talk ourselves out of it, we find excuses, we lose motivation, we give up. We've yet to meet a person who doesn't struggle with this spectrum of being ready for self-improvement and facing resistance—no matter how well the instruction manual was written about how to achieve their goals.

In fact, even being given instructions to do something differently plays a role in resistance.

Let's play a game to demonstrate how many of us react to being told what to do.

> *First Instruction:* Raise your hand as high as you can. Keep it raised.

> *Second Instruction:* With your hand still raised. Raise it up even more.

See! You had room to raise it even higher! The first direction was to raise it as high as you could . . . but you probably didn't. You unconsciously resisted. Your mind likes to play the game of *least effort* as a default behavior, exerting little to help you actually change.

Where are you on the spectrum of readiness to resistance when it comes to changing how you show up in the relationship and adopting a new communication style? Even when you think the gap is a canyon to cross or that it is the other party's problem, lack of skills, and/or immaturity that is responsible? Will you choose to show up clean and curious and engage in a new paradigm to release you both out of the finger trap?

We coached Michael from the Drama Triangle in the last chapter. We gave him instructions. We offered proven strategies on how he could be successful and retire strong with an amazing legacy. We showed him how to disrupt his reactions. We showed him how to shift his kaleidoscope to see Trent's value as a younger designer with an eye for new markets and updated classic traditions, like bow ties. We gave him tools to lead with curiosity in nearly all his interactions with Trent to try and find ways to understand, like, and respect him. We even told him what to say and how to say it. None of it mattered. He never showed up clean and authentically curious in his interactions with Trent, and eventually, others in the office. Michael was committed to keep a canyon between them.

We all know how that ended. Michael was unable to close the gap between resistance and readiness. He was unable to improve his relationship with Trent, which subsequently impacted nearly all his relationships at work because he tried to pull his friends and allies into the Drama Triangle with him. At every turn, when presented with a way to change, Michael resisted all instructions. His pride won and he paid a hefty price.

The lessons here are:

1. *Please don't be as obstinate as Michael.* His life was miserable in the finger trap and entirely avoidable. He was the great conductor of his own unnecessary suffering. He harmed Trent, colleagues, and the business . . . and for what? More suffering.

2. *Only you can move yourself on the spectrum of resistance to readiness.* Evaluate what gap you need to personally close to move you to a state of readiness, where you can accept instruction and commit to changing behavior.

3. *Instructions only work if you commit to giving them a fair shot.* Your brain and mind and body will likely resist new ways of saying or doing things.

Disrupting the invisible forces and your habitual reactions takes diligent effort. Are you ready to release yourself from the finger trap? Great! Let's learn some tactics to disrupt the invisible forces, so that you can show up clean and curious to communicate better and bridge the gap.

PROVEN TACTICS TO SHOW UP CLEAN

What does it mean to show up clean?

1. You choose to disrupt the hijack of those invisible forces.
2. Your intention is pure—you truly want to improve the relationship.

We live in the pressure cooker of life in our human suits. Stress, anxiety, and pressure is constant in our professional world. This means that it's easy to be hijacked, often, and potentially several times a day. So, you need a bag of proven tactics that you can employ immediately—in the middle of your workday—to protect your bubble-gum-colored prefrontal cortex from the dark clouds of AMY's chemical spew. You don't have 26 hours to lose in one single hijack, right?

You have to be an *awareness ninja* to keep your executive function—communication, curiosity, creativity, and decision-making skills—optimal and ready for whatever you face.

To that end, we call the following list of on-the-spot tactics *biology disruption tools* because they interrupt default, biologically embedded reactions that your system has built over your lifetime.

Each tactic is simple and has an accompanying wealth of research to prove it works. It's likely you've seen, heard, and/or read about these tools before. Here's a note of warning: if you're still searching for a "silver bullet" after reading the list then you missed the point. Simple strategies, when practiced and used throughout your workday, will be the game changer in how you show up clean to better connect, communicate, and collaborate across any gap you face.

Here's some instructions you might want to resist: Try each one at least ten times before your Inner Narrator creates a story about why it doesn't work and convinces you to give up on what's possible. Embrace a technique that is new to you or, better yet, dive deep into what worked in the past. You are unique and some may work better than others. Be curious about what shifts when you commit to practicing one or more of these techniques.

BREATHE[2]

You open your email on Monday morning and are greeted by an inbox full of demands. Your boss has surprised you with three important calls on your calendar, all before 10 a.m. and a slide deck to complete by noon. To top it off, you were up in the middle of the night with a fussy baby. You're not only exhausted but overwhelmed and irritated. Your thoughts are jumbled, you're not even sure where to start or how to respond to people waiting for your replies. What to say that won't come off as whiny or annoyed?

When your mind cannot grab a single thought or is raging and looping about something or someone . . . shift all of your focus to counting your breaths and feeling the oxygen move in and out. Intentional breathing, the kind where you pay close attention, slows your heart rate, decreasing the flow of agitating chemicals to your brain and helping to keep your executive function running smoothly. Counting your breaths internally provides your mind with an activity to do rather than distracting you with a triggered Inner Narrator. Research shows that there are exponential health benefits to breathing in through your nose and then out through your mouth, and there is a "magic" number of seconds for how long you hold and release. Aim to breathe in for 5.5 seconds through your nose, drawing air into your lungs and belly, then out for 5.5 seconds through your mouth.

You close your email. Set a timer on your phone for two minutes. Close your eyes. Let the weight of your body settle into your chair. You close your mouth and breathe through your nostrils. In for 5.5 seconds and exhale out your mouth for 5.5 seconds. Repeat for two minutes. As you do, soften your jaw. Soften your shoulders. When the phone chimes after two minutes open your eyes, sit up. Decide what to respond to first, based on importance and deadline. Let go of any desire that you need a clean inbox and must respond to everyone at this moment. Let the frantic pressure inside—and outside—subside. Make a list of what you can accomplish and breathe through each to-do without being hijacked.

STOP LABELING. BE A MOVIE CAMERA

You walk out of a s@%tstorm of a meeting. As the chief revenue officer, responsible for the sales team, you just witnessed your entire team implode with excuses. Your top two sales leaders are threatening to leave, and each have headhunters knocking at their door. The gauntlet has been thrown. They both say they will walk if changes aren't made within 30 days. Their demands are stupid, unreasonable, and frankly, impossible, given your resources. You are scared about them leaving, but also pissed at being held hostage to their demands. Where is the respect that you deserve after being so generous last year with their bonuses? You walk to your office and say to your secretary, "What a s@%tshow," then pull your door closed. It slams—you didn't mean it to—but upon hearing it, you realize how livid you've become.

Words create worlds. In this case, labeling the situation as a "s@%tstorm" is akin to blowing hot air into an already raging wildfire. It's why you accidently slammed the door instead of just pulling it shut.

Your human suit is already wired to dichotomize, to split things into buckets that are labeled good/bad, smart/dumb, black/white. Assessing and judging situations and/or people is partially tied to AMY. Labeling is part of our biology, connected to an unconscious survival mechanism that assesses things as a way to know how to safely interact with them.

The key is to detach from labeling people or situations with hyperbolic or strong emotional language. To do so, we suggest using the *movie camera method*. Try to gain psychological distance from the situation and step outside of your emotions, reflect on what happened but only through the lens of a movie camera. Witness yourself as a character and the others in the scene with you, too. The caveat is that you can't see, hear, or know any of characters' interior worlds, including your own. You can only see actions and hear uttered words. Depersonalize it and be factual about what you witness. Override any desire that allows drama and toxic emotions to trump logic.

The door slams and it makes you flinch. You sigh and throw your padfolio on your desk. *Get it under control,* you berate yourself. You stand and lean against your desk, arms crossed. You breathe. Close your eyes and become a movie camera. You see a team with disappointed faces. You hear people getting lost as they fight over semantics. You see two leaders struggling to both manage and motivate this disappointed team. You see them asking for help from you. You see yourself. You look annoyed. At one point, you're arguing back and clearly not listening. Then you see it, the moment you labeled it a s@%tstorm: you folded your arms and steeled your eyes. Then you walked out.

You ask yourself: *Was it really a s@%tstorm or did I make it more awful by giving up in my own frustration and labeling it as such? In the movie camera, I see two leaders and a team struggling because they don't have enough direction and/or resources.* You tell yourself, *these situations happen all the time. They aren't s@%tstorms; they are recoverable.* You open your eyes, take your seat, and write on your pad: *Who do I need to be to my team and what is the best outcome I can achieve in this situation?*

FIND SILENCE AND SPACE

The week has been a whirlwind of meetings and complicated decisions about a blocked and inconsistent supply chain that has created a negative domino effect in your industry. You, and many others, are not able to deliver upon contracts and/or promises made to your clients. Everyone is feeling the pressure and suffering. It's a global, complex issue, and really nobody is at fault—yet your team and customers are caught in the Drama Triangle trying to find who to blame. You want to lead with personal responsibility and help the situation, especially for your people . . . who are quickly turning against you. You feel foggy and frustrated at the external conditions causing all this turmoil and want to yell, "It's not my fault!"

When you are under this much pressure confusion can take over quickly—especially with problems that include many people. Gaining greater clarity between the root of the problem and the innovative solution often requires silence and space. Instead of rushing to find the fix or assign the blame, choose to be in an uncertain "in-between place," where the problem and a solution have yet to be matched. The in-between place is where silence exists. Space and silence are often uncomfortable for people because it requires giving up a belief that all things are in our control. Releasing control often makes people panic—and that triggers AMY.

The truth is that brilliant things happen in the in-between space—in a silent, spacious, and calm mind.

A spacious and calm mind is a place where you can wait for what hasn't yet been revealed. It's where you trust that the beginnings of a solution will appear. Gaining space and silence creates the conditions of a spacious and calm mind to explore mindful meditation and/or prayer. Both approaches create those special "in-between" spaces for new ideas, thoughts, perspectives, and solutions to emerge.

Mindful meditation is an approach used to be conscious about the thoughts that enter your head and let them go, one by one, as you clear your mind of all thoughts and simply be.[3] This type of meditation initiates a "relaxation response."[4]

Prayer is another way to create space in the middle of a challenge. Prayer can be a way to call on your connection to God and access an understanding beyond your human suit. You surrender your control and ask for wisdom, guidance, patience, and grace from beyond the storm. You listen for a Word in the silence.

You sit in your car, alone. Nobody can hear or see you. You set your phone timer for ten minutes. You close your eyes and visualize sitting inside a snow globe. In the snow globe, you look up to the dome-shaped sky where each of your thoughts drift like flakes. You allow each thought to fall and dissipate. You are not allowed to gather the flakes or make snowballs with your falling thoughts. You merely sit and watch the snow fall until you're distracted by something else in the snow globe—the beautiful weather, the sounds of birds, the smell of flowers. Soon enough, it's quiet. No more flakes are falling.

If you choose to pray—you surrender to God and ask to be given new clarity, understanding, a shift of perspective, a way to get through the blockage. You listen in the silence. Soon, a word, an idea, a name, or a new thought might appear. The phone chimes. You're refreshed and invigorated. You have a pivot or an idea.

THROW A PRIVATE TEMPER TANTRUM

The sky is falling. People suck. You were passed over for the promotion, again. Your marriage is in shambles. Why can't you just be a hermit? That disgusting coworker won't stop eating with their mouth open. Eff this. You're not going to obey. They don't own you.

You have a right to feel anger. So, scream. Throw stuff. Cuss. Punch a bag. Slam a stuffed bag against the wall a gazillion times. Whatever you do, release the hounds, because if you choose to keep all that rage inside, it will soon go deep and become part of your bones. Your body keeps score over time.[5] Anger, stress, and toxic emotions will gradually eat away at your health and spirit if you do not let them release. The soured Inner Narrator will remind you later and amplify the pain. These feelings must go somewhere.

You lock yourself in a closet, a bathroom, the car. You scream as loud as you can without alarming people. You may have to use a mophead, a wad of toilet paper, a wadded-up shirt or scarf to muffle the sound. You cuss out whomever you need to in your head until the pressure valve is released and blowing off steam. Then, you shake it off—literally. You flail and wiggle and shake out each limb—feeling your skin jiggle. You feel better after having your reaction elsewhere, and alone.

CALL ON YOUR PERSONAL BOARD OF DIRECTORS[6]

It is Sunday night at 6 p.m. and you and your business partner have just spent the better part of a strategic weekend retreat in a blow-up fight about the business's budget and spending habits. Accusations have been leveled. Ugly words used. Threats exchanged. You both fabricated evidence to make your point. To make things even worse, you must wake up in the morning and deliver a pitch to a new prospect. You can't even see how you are going to be able to show up for this important meeting you both have been preparing for over the past month. It feels like it is all falling apart, and, honestly, your partner is to blame since he is the one who started the fight, full well knowing that you both have a big day tomorrow. You pull out your phone and call Susan—a mentor who has been in your shoes.

There is nothing like a conversation with someone who—and this is important—has the skills to help you to process and call you into a fuller picture of truth. In fact, we suggest that you cultivate a Personal Board of Directors, three to four people who can be called upon to keep you on track when fights like this threaten to derail crucial relationships (as well as support and advise you during nontumultuous times). We suggest you identify the following people:

1. *A Mentor.* Choose a person who knows what you're capable of and is able to coach you to use your gifts, strengths, and skills to make the situation better.
2. *A Role Model.* Choose a person who inspires you and has the type of character that you aspire to inhabit. Talk to them and ask *what would you do?*
3. *An Encouraging Friend.* Choose a person who knows you—your backstory, your ambitions, your flaws. Talk it out—vent, process, and let your friend cheer you up.
4. *A Coach.* Choose a person who intimidates you a bit and can keep you accountable. This person doesn't have to be your boss, or a boss, just someone who is tough, can call you out, and keep your feet to the fire.

Susan reminds you that work partners are like spouses and divorcing your "work hubby" over this would be disastrous and ruin years of work. She offers a story about when she and her own "work wife" had a falling out and what it took to glue their relationship back together. You feel less alone. She helps you focus on what matters, providing you with evidence about how you've managed conflict in the past. She holds you capable and accountable to show up on Monday morning with clean energy to be with them during the presentation—because that will make an impression on the clients that you're hoping to sign. You and Susan hang up and you send a text message to your work hubby before midnight. "I'm sorry I was a jerk. I enjoy and respect our business and relationship. I'm still here for you. And I know you're here for me. Let's not let today's fight mess up our energy tomorrow—I'm looking forward to nailing the presentation. We have a lot going for us. We will work it out. See you in the morning."

FREE WRITE[7]

It is time for your annual review. Next week, you are meeting your boss to explore your 360 feedback and begin drafting your own, required, personal self-evaluation. You spent the weekend stewing on the feedback you received from the 360. You resonate with some of the comments, but a few really sting. You are hurt by a few sentences that you feel are completely off base and out of left field. You also are unclear about what you want to take personal responsibility for in your own self-evaluative process. You intended to ask for a 5 percent raise and now are doubting yourself.

Writing anything that has to be turned in and evaluated places us under pressure. Add negative criticism or critical feedback from others and things can go south fast. Whenever you're hijacked by pressure or self-doubt and the thoughts are swimming—don't be afraid of the pen! Pick it up and start to write. Allow yourself to write—even the worst junk. Spill all those terrible thoughts onto the page. Nobody has to see them. They don't even have to make sense. You can destroy it later if you want (which sometimes feels terrific!). Journaling, writing, and expressing yourself on paper is cheap therapy. It allows you to see patterns in your thinking, too, and make connections that didn't occur to you before.

You set a timer for ten minutes and scribble out everything that appears in your mind. You don't try to make logical sense of the criticism. You don't even use correct grammar or spelling. You write in your natural voice and words finally become unstuck and start flowing. You begin articulating your contributions, strengths, and talents. You feel okay now to address the 360 feedback and can even see how your strengths can sometimes work against you. For instance, you notice in your free write that your ability to pay attention to details is echoed in a criticism about how you get lost in the "minutiae of the process, which can drag the team down." You have an AHA! You come up with language to address that in your personal self-evaluation: "While it may seem that I'm hypersensitive to how documents are processed, what I'm really trying to do is save the team time by getting the details correct the first time, and that means we need to pay attention to the process itself."

PRACTICE GRATITUDE

You are the social media manager for a growing dental office group. The social media you invested in has had a huge return. You're crushing it. The phones are ringing off the hook with new patients looking to be seen. You can't keep up. While you and the five dentists are thrilled, the front office staff is overwhelmed. At first it was okay—they were excited about the new clients. But now that they have to create new files, get medical records, coordinate insurances, and process new patient forms . . . they feel disrespected by how much work has come their way. Your desk is near theirs, so it's not like you can ignore them. And some of them are your friends who you happy hour with. Over drinks, one of them blamed you "jokingly" for making them so stressed out. So, it seems that the solution you were looking for, new patients, has now become a problem. The five big bosses say, "This is a great problem to have!" And they're right, but the complaint from the other direction is getting you down and now it's all you can focus on—and that's impacting your relationship with them.

The Greater Good Science Center at University of California, Berkeley, has researched the psychological and health benefits of practicing gratitude.[8] When things are going truly great, or even when they really aren't, you can interrupt feeling down or blue by practicing gratitude. You can make a mental list, or write it down. Recognize everything for which you are grateful—and small things count, even that cup of morning coffee. Don't forget to also find gratitude for the problem you're in. When framed as a problem, it will tear you down; however, if framed as a gift, you can find the learning and gratitude for the issue. So, the next time your Inner Narrator is lit up with gripes, shift your focus to what you can be grateful for. It's a mood improver!

You write the following across the top of a notepad: *Thank you sun, morning coffee, internet, and chocolate donuts. I am grateful to create fun memes, videos, and posts as part of my job. Thank you teeth that need to be straightened, whitened, cleaned, and fixed. I am grateful for the dentists. I am grateful for the staff. Thank you Melanie for showing me how successful my tips, tricks, and aesthetic turned out to be. Thank you new clients for paying attention to our feed.*

PRACTICE FORGIVENESS[9]

You look at next week's schedule in the back office before closing up shop. Your schedule is jacked. Out of the blue. You know that the clothing store where you work needs more staff. You feel like you have given all your creativity to this owner and now she has completely blindsided you by changing your schedule and giving the new girl all the good shifts where people actually buy stuff. You walk out the door, beyond confused and lost. That night you toss and turn and fight and argue with your boss all night in a quasi-dreamland that is exhausting.

We all face moments where we struggle to respect the decision of someone we work for. One strategy to employ is the gift of forgiveness. Forgiveness is a conscious decision to surrender the feelings of rage or resentment toward a person, or group (or even yourself), who has harmed you, regardless of their response. Forgiveness is most often a process—it is ongoing—and not a single action or event.

In the workplace, there will be plenty of times to practice forgiveness. At some point or another, you will fail and disappoint someone. Or someone will fail and disappoint you. Pain and frustrations are guaranteed in relationships. However, how long you choose to suffer and remain in that state of pain is up to you. Forgiveness can wiggle you out of the finger trap because it frees you from struggling and engaging in suffering. True forgiveness shuts the pain down and lets it go. It's just as much for you as it is for them or in service of the relationship as a whole.

Forgiveness shifts you to a more meaningful and productive place. Research confirms that unresolved emotions come at a high cost. Forgiveness is a process that resolves those emotions and keeps us from reliving painful or confusing events.

You get out of bed and make coffee before calling a meeting with your boss to discuss the schedule, new girl, and your impacted commission. As you sip and yawn, you ask yourself what you really want. Do you want your old shifts? Do you want a good relationship with your boss? Do you truly like working at that clothing store? All the answers are yes. You realize that yelling, blaming, shaming, and being mad at your boss is not going to get you what you want. You sip more coffee and think. A voice says, *"Maybe there's a reason why she did that. You could decide to ask instead of being mad at them."* You tussle with this idea as you drink more coffee, but the more you tussle the worse you feel. So you listen to the voice and choose forgiveness. You tell yourself, "I am forgiving her" and draw a line in the sand. As you're showering, intrusive thoughts begin again, and you disrupt them by saying, "I am forgiving her." When you walk into work you feel clear and confident that you can address this with your boss without having a tone in your voice.

RECITE A REPOSITIONING SENTENCE, AFFIRMATION, OR GUIDING MANTRA

Don't say the wrong thing. Don't say the wrong thing. Crap . . . all you can think about is not saying the wrong thing. You better not blow it, or your colleague will never speak to you again. She's had it with you, that's clear. You start to feel sweaty and tight. You can't stop looping over the fear you're going to say the wrong thing or freeze and have nothing to say at all.

The minute you feel pressure and the Inner Narrator poke you, break the pattern. Interject with a verbal and powerful statement of a personal, aspirational truth that you believe.[10] Speak it out loud. It is critical that this statement be prepared in advance and have a repositioning nature to its language. This statement should pull you away from whatever you're obsessing about or labeling negatively. For example, a person who struggles with constant worry might have one of these repositioning statements:

- "Contentment is a choice."
- "I am calm, safe, and grateful."
- "Things can change for the better—in a second."

You lock yourself in the office bathroom and look in the mirror. "I am prepared to share and contribute." You look yourself in the eye. "I am prepared to share and contribute." You say it as you exit the bathroom and down the hall, but this time internally. You show up to your meeting, you sit down and give yourself a moment to breathe, and begin.

PINCH YOUR THUMB OR RUB A ROCK

You are about to get on stage at your annual meeting to propose a new curriculum. It is fairly straightforward, and you have prepared well, but you're anxious about public speaking and taking questions. You look around and everyone else seems to be fine. That makes you more nervous. You get antsy and look longingly at the door, wanting to flee. Your nerves are getting the best of you.

When you struggle to lessen AMY's impact and are flooded with anxiety, fidget with something. Seriously! Fidget toys, worry stones, and other sensory toys that distract us are beyond the hype. Research shows that they work for both kids and adults. So, stick a small rock in your pocket to rub or fidget with and center your focus. Carry it with you and when pressure hits, fidget. If you don't have a rock or think that's silly—try this amazing trick: bring your hands close together and pinch one of your thumbs. Hard. It's a public speaking trick that many people use to stay grounded when they are nervous.

Dammit! You forgot your worry stone at home. You center in your seat and pinch your thumb. You look around. Nobody can see; it just looks like your hands are together. With each worry you pinch harder, until you're focusing on the pulsating nerves in your thumb. Soon time is up and you're on stage. When the questions come, you struggle a bit at first to block out the nervous noise in your head, but pinching your thumb keeps you focused on what they are saying. Afterward, even though you stumbled a little, you are happy to admit that it went better than expected.

MOVE

For weeks, you've been sitting at your desk finishing up the master HR handbook. Hours and hours of sitting and refreshing job descriptions, policies, and procedures has been mind numbing. Your lunch hour arrives, and you spend it like normal: scrolling through your phone catching up on your social media and news. You notice that Brad, the insurance rep two offices down, has posted a ton of obnoxious memes about the upcoming election. You two have consistently warred over politics, and this election has proven to be divisive and polarizing. You're completely offended by his jokes, sarcasm, and political cartoons that debase your candidate. You decide to go down to his office and give him a piece of your mind.

We stagnate throughout the day, similar to a small pond of water sitting under a hot sun. The water gets stale and murky because there's no air or flow to cycle it. The same thing happens inside our bodies—we sit too long and our juices stew. We were born to move and get the blood flowing again.

Anaerobic exercise[11] forces your body to demand more energy than your aerobic system can produce, creating a dramatic shift to your blood flow. Being in increased motion changes your response to emotion and pressure. Combining this with one of the other techniques can be a powerful disrupter. Basically—exercise! Move your body however you can. Go for a walk, a run. Jog standing up. Dance. Stretch. Shake it off.

Turns out, Brad is not in his office. You start to return to your office, but see light shining through the front door. Instead of returning to your desk and scrolling, you choose to go for a brisk walk. You soak up the sunshine, make a few rounds in the business complex, and soon enough you've forgotten about Brad's social media entirely. You clear your head (and lungs) and return to the office ready to finish the darn HR handbook.

DISRUPTION EQUALS EVENTUAL CHANGE

In most situations, people are doing the best that they can with the knowledge and skills they can access in the moment that they are experiencing. That is why having a bag of on-the-spot *biology disruption* tactics is so important. When you practice them regularly, you can access them more quickly in pressure-filled moments. In addition, these tactics can help you move from a place of resistance to readiness to movement in your relationships. Releasing the pressure and stopping the hijack moves the needle.

> ➤ **Another Big Aha!** ◄
>
> Small daily shifts make all the difference in how you show up to connect, communicate, and collaborate. Your brain is malleable, and disrupting your reactions with these strategies is how you begin rewiring habitual behaviors that keep you from showing up clean.

Give *biology disruption* a solid, working chance before you give up because, frankly, AMY and a soured Inner Narrator wants to keep you safe in your bubble of normal. Offer grace to yourself as you try these new techniques—even when they feel silly or stupid.

REFLECTION QUESTIONS

- Where might you extend more grace to yourself and others as you remember people are doing the best they can with the skills they can access when under the pressure they are experiencing?
- Where are you on the spectrum of readiness to resistance when it comes to showing up clean with a person with whom you struggle?
- Do you currently have a simple, on-the-spot strategy to disrupt the invisible forces that threaten to hijack you from being communicative or connective?

ACTION ITEM
The Choice: Disrupt over Hijack

Choose one biology disruption strategy and implement it for a few days. Write it down. Plan out how you will use it. Schedule it. Practice it. Practice with effort.

JOIN THE CONVERSATION AND INTERACT ONLINE
#disruptthehijack

SHOW UP CURIOUS
Be an Explorer and Choose to Care

This chapter is about showing up curious and choosing to care about others in spite of obstacles and pressure. This next part is "in living color," exemplifying what you've learned in the previous chapters while walking you through a one-day event we designed for an organization that needed to bridge a tremendous gap. We want to show you how we flipped the traditional script to bring together people who are full of distrust and polarized—unable to make critical decisions with any sense of unity. Our aim was to shift them to a place where a new level of curiosity and care could be enacted for one another so that they could connect, communicate, and collaborate more effectively.

HELPING AN ENTIRE ORGANIZATION BRIDGE THE GAP: A CASE STUDY

Welcome to a well-known healthcare association's annual one-day retreat, where their political action committee was convening to finalize their giving and endorsement strategy for the year. In full transparency, the healthcare association didn't truly hire us for our human dynamics' expertise. The association chose us because we matched the issue of what it was facing: political polarization and distrust found within a dueling two-party system.

Remember: we are "work-wives" who couldn't be more different from the outside looking in: Republican/Democrat; country/ rock 'n' roll; upper class/working class; suburban/urban. We mirror a growing and concerning schism within this association and in many workplaces across the nation. We practice what we teach and use many of the strategies and tools in this book to bridge the numerous gaps between us and keep working.

This healthcare association convenes medical professionals to network, learn, and collaborate. Its membership covered a diverse range within their field of medicine. We were hired to work with the association's PAC representatives, who were struggling to make decisions about which lawmakers and elected officials to support with their political action dollars at both state and federal levels. These thirty-five "delegates" were elected by membership to represent regions throughout their state, one of the largest in the United States. What made the delegates' decisions heated and difficult was that the nation had experienced a year of seemingly nonstop trauma from January 2020 to January 2021: a global pandemic, racial injustice and civic unrest, a polarizing election, and the protest and events that transpired at the Capitol on January 6, 2021.

The healthcare association and its PAC delegation had run into a serious problem. Their delegates had retreated into their political parties of red versus blue, conservatives versus progressives, Republicans versus Democrats. They were struggling to understand, like, and/or respect one another given the heated state of current events and the job placed before them.

The association's executive director and leadership team had tried to manage the various perspectives, voices, and opinions on their own, and unfortunately, at every turn, the delegates turned on each other—which slid them right into the Drama Triangle. Fighting, shame and blame, victimhood, and toxic rhetoric were damaging something that could be amazing: their collective power to improve standards in their industry. In addition, there was little "glue" to hold the delegation together. The delegates worked mostly in isolation and simply didn't see each other enough to know one another and therefore didn't have a solid foundation of trust and respect to bolster their relationships while under pressure and when difficult decisions needed to be made.

> ## ➤ The Big Aha! ◄
>
> Quality relationships are built on a foundation of mutual trust and respect, which helps us "care" about the other when conflict has naturally triggered AMY and soured Inner Narrators. When there is a lack of trust and respect, it's super-easy to stay siloed and not really care about teamwork, unity, or bridging the gap.

Time was of essence. Decisions about their strategic political action dollars needed to be finalized . . . and the delegates were fed up with one another and deadlocked. The split was pretty much 50/50, and nobody would budge from either side to achieve bipartisanship. Now, they could have easily split the pot of money equally among lawmakers and elected officials, yet that didn't feel true to the task they were assigned: *Donate political action dollars strategically to solve problems and create positive impact in the healthcare industry.* Leadership felt that divvying out the dollars wouldn't move any needle forward on legislative issues that were negatively affecting their industry.

The healthcare association dilemmas echo an issue affecting most workplaces. Polarization is real and growing within our offices and work lives. This divisiveness comes at a high cost to companies and organizations, no matter how large or small. Because of our human suit, people's personal and professional values and beliefs are stitched together in interesting ways and not easily discarded when we enter the workplace. Dialogues about race, class, politics, gender, and economics are woven into the fabric of daily life and rarely sequestered to just our personal lives. These conversations greet us at the water cooler, the conference table, and during happy hours. Very few leaders and offices are equipped to deal with the fallout when polarization and heated emotional disagreements enter work relationships.

The Society of Human Resource Management (SHRM) found that nearly one in five Americans quit their jobs in the last five years due to a toxic workplace, costing US companies roughly $223 billion. SHRM's report[1] suggests that political conflicts at work will continue to drive disengagement and intensify toxicity that makes employees quit. The data is quite startling—and please note that it was conducted *before* the nation went through the great dumpster fire of 2020:

- 42 percent of employees have personally experienced political disagreements in the workplace.
- 56 percent say politics and the discussion of political issues has become more common in the past four years.
- 34 percent say their workplace is *not* inclusive of differing political perspectives.

Today, companies are racing to figure out best practices and strategies to address turnover and toxic work environments while creating more inclusive and diverse work environments. And the consistent aspiration that we hear from our clients is this: *We want everyone at the table, including the leader, to be able to engage meaningfully in discussions that often challenge deeply held beliefs, opinions, and personal values.*

As facilitators, the questions we think about are:

- How do you get people who are resistant, fed up, and/or stubborn to open their minds and ears to hear a different perspective and care?
- How do you get people to show up clean enough to engage meaningfully? To set aside their fury, moodiness, snark, and/ or passive-aggressiveness? To set aside their victimhood, sadness, doubt, and frustration?
- How do you get someone who is so certain with their facts and education to disarm their knowledge, quit with being smug, and hear something new that may contextualize or deepen what they think they know?

Well, first, we must assess if we're dealing with a gap or a canyon. For example, the biggest canyon we see is when one side has harmed the other with malicious intent and discrimination. Those canyons can be crossed, with HR, professional mediators, and/or lawyers, but it's above our—and likely your—paygrade.

So in our preparation for the facilitation, we asked leadership at the healthcare association: "Has anyone filed a formal complaint or lawsuit on the board against anyone who serves, including your team?"

They looked at us beleaguered: "No. It hasn't gone *that* far."

"Great! That means there are probably not any canyons to cross, just gaps to bridge. We can do that." Jennifer said.

Then Katie asked, "Do you experience delegates struggling to understand, like, and/or respect the beliefs, opinions, and decisions of some of their fellow delegates?"

They nodded their heads; some said yes. Mostly we were met with faces that screamed: *DUH.*

"Great. We just want to be clear about the root of what you're up against, instead of focusing solely on the political disagreements." Jennifer smiled.

Katie asked, "We know that you have limited time—only one day—did you have any thoughts about the agenda before we design the day's activities?"

The big boss answered, "We thought you would be the perfect people to facilitate a debate between the two parties and support them as they hash this out. We assume that Katie will lead the Democrats and Jennifer will lead the Republicans. We thought there'd be a two-hour working lunch where you'll both be with your individual teams to help them create their own presentation. Then you two will facilitate the debate in the afternoon with room for dialogue and questions. After that, the delegates will cast their votes, privately, and we'll be able to allocate the funds and call it a day."

A debate? We looked at each other, took a deep breath, and responded, "We hear your goal: give an opportunity for sides to be heard, information to be shared, opinions to be offered, and values to be "fought" for. Good goal, and in our experience, when emotions are high and people are dug in, this approach won't work. Research shows that humans, when under siege of their values being compromised, can't actually listen well enough to understand or hear something new. They have already made up their minds based on the information they trust and the evidence that they've accumulated through their unique, lived experiences. The energetic structure of a debate could set up further division because it assumes that to win, one must battle out their argument manipulating whatever they can use to convince people to choose their side. Your delegates are smart and clever. We guarantee that each side will put forth its best speaker—someone who can use emotion, story, data, and facts to be highly persuasive. Placing your thirty-five delegates into a debate dynamic is not going to yield a different outcome. Your delegates will reach an impasse, again. You may as well split your pot of money evenly across lawmakers."

"Then what do you suggest?"

"Let's flip the script. Let's design a morning of learning and activities to bring forth what is missing in this delegation: curiosity and care. Then, and only then, will we break up the group to prepare thoughtful mini-speeches. Each of us will take one side for a few hours to support them for engaging in an afternoon of values-driven storytelling before they cast their vote."

"Good luck," The big boss said. "Half the folks in there won't buy any fluff."

We smiled. "Nor would we."

SETTING UP THE MORNING WORKSHOP

Given that we had them for only one day, we didn't have enough time with the delegation to introduce the science of the brain and mind, relational dynamics in the Drama Triangle, or biology disruption tactics for showing up clean. It didn't really matter, though: the delegates, as far as we knew, were already hijacked and stuck in the finger trap.

They weren't going to show up clean.

So we took another approach. We wanted every delegate to have enough concern and care in their heart and mind to silence their Inner Narrator and listen to a unique, and potentially new, perspective before they cast their vote. Finally, each delegate would be invited to share their story without pointing fingers, using belittling language, or making grand assumptions and judgments about the other side.

In a normal year, teaching curiosity is an interactive, engaging exercise that helps argumentative adults bridge the gap quicker than most other interventions. Curiosity-driven experiences do a terrific job of shifting the naysayers from resistance to readiness in their ability to communicate and collaborate across the gap. Due to COVID-19, we ran this workshop virtually.

Social psychologists at the University of California, Irvine, New York University, and the University of Toronto[2] found that when adults experience curiosity, wonder, and awe, they diminish their ego and individual concerns and increase prosocial behavior. And it makes sense from the standpoint of our neurochemistry because participating in curiosity-driven experiences often floods us with a feel-good chemical cocktail of dopamine and serotonin. Ultimately, when you show up curious, you can better quiet the soured Inner Narrator, subdue AMY's impact, and open to work collaboratively.

Here's how the morning played out with the delegates.

WELCOME: HOW ARE YOU SHOWING UP, TODAY?

We welcomed the delegates to the Bridge the Gap experience by asking them how they were showing up to today's event. On the screen, we asked them to choose, privately, which role they were embodying[3] this morning:

- *Explorer:* Curious and ready to go on an adventure into the wild unknown
- *Knower:* Knowledgeable and prepared with my own information and experiences
- *Tourist:* Excited to take a break from work and see the sites portrayed on the brochure
- *Voyeur:* Let's see how this plays out, someone go fetch the buttered popcorn
- *Prisoner:* Forced to be here, no choice

We asked, "If you could choose to be any of these roles today, which one would you choose and why?" Resoundingly, most played along and chose Explorer and Tourist (like good students). Some admitted with honesty that they wished they could adopt the Explorer or Tourist roles, yet they had lost energy and/or hope to show up with optimism. We thanked them for their honesty. Then we explained the difference between Explorer and Tourist:

- An Explorer knowingly goes on an adventure with ups and downs and with the expectation and hope that they'll discover something new and valuable.
- A Tourist is like an Explorer; however, they come with expectations, wanting to taste, touch, and experience the glossy stuff that was promised on the brochure. That doesn't mean a Tourist can't stumble upon the unexpected; it's just less likely.

Katie began, "Today, we possibly have some tough and anxious conversations ahead of us, and we propose using a new perspective to navigate through them. Here's a metaphor to create some shared understanding of what's in store for our day together. We are going on a "hike" through a beautiful, high-altitude mountain. As we hike, as we have these conversations, on the mountain, together, there will be steep cliffs, rattlesnakes, and blisters on our toes. We'll also experience beautiful vistas and surprising wildlife. At moments on the hike, and in conversation, you'll likely feel angry, alone, and tired. Many of you might want to quit. If you can all stick together as a team, then everyone will make it up and down the mountain safely—but only if we take care of each other along the path."

Then Jennifer asked, "What will it take for you to step fully into the Explorer role as we make our way through the treacherous landscape of deciding who gets your hard-earned money?" Some answers were:

- "Let go of the past and see with new eyes."
- "Join the adventure and participate."
- "Be ready—and willing—to discover something new."

Jennifer pressed the team further: "Terrific! We would love for this to happen. Are there more actionable ways for us to be Explorers, together? Be honest."

RULES OF ENGAGEMENT: NO BUTS, ONLY ANDS

Jennifer continued: "For instance, how will you engage as an Explorer on the team if someone takes you in a direction that makes you uncomfortable? How will you be an Explorer when someone points out something harmless and you see it as a danger? Or vice versa? How will you engage when you want to throw certain people off the cliff because they annoy or anger you? What about when someone tries to push you off the cliff?"

Katie added, "I'm assuming that each of you wants a positive experience today, where you can gather more information about how to cast your vote. To do that, we need some rules of engagement."

Common rules appeared around putting away distractions and keeping cameras on so that people could be present and engaged. A few important ones arose:

- Assume positive intent when people speak or ask questions.
- Don't dominate the conversation.
- No sidebars, private jokes, or rude comments.
- Depersonalize things that make you, personally, feel attacked.

Then we added our personal favorite: No *buts*, only *ands*.

Immediately, a woman asked, "What does that mean?"

Jennifer said, "I'm so glad you asked. Every time you want to say *but,* see if you can replace it with an *and.*"

Katie offered this example: "I love having Facebook because it connects me to my friends and family, *but* I detest all the political memes and attacks in my feed lately. Versus: I love having Facebook because it connects me to my friends and family, *and* I detest all the political memes and attacks in my feed lately."

"Maybe I'm missing the point, but why does that matter?" one guy asked. "Aren't you expressing the same thing?"

Jennifer responded, "Great question! Do you hear in the first *'but'* statement that the political memes and attacks trump the love she has for seeing her friends and family online? The word *'but'* places two related thoughts into a competition where typically the latter thought 'wins.' Usually, the latter thought is negative— which keeps people feeling defeated, depressed, and angered. So, when you intentionally include *'and'* in your sentences, you're lessening the competition between two thoughts that could exist harmoniously in the same sentence. This tiny shift has immense impact on how you communicate with people."[4]

As an additional example, we typed the following sentences into the chat and asked them to read them aloud and hear the difference:

- I agree with you that the protestors should bear responsibility for breaking into the Capitol, *but* what do you think about the behavior of the president that day?
- I agree with you that the protestors should bear responsibility for breaking into the Capitol *and* what do you think about the behavior of the president that day?

Katie then asked, "What shifted in the sentence, in terms of tone? How might someone respond differently to each question? Will they play defense because of the word *but* or might they feel 'invited' into a conversation about the behavior of the president with the word *and*? The word *but* energetically introduces conflict into the statement,[5] and if we want to bridge the gap and have better relationships and communication, then we might want to eliminate unnecessary competition because that shoves us into debate mode. We're not debating today."

Let's pause and review this further in your everyday work scenarios. Look at what shifts:

- "Stacey, I want to go over your feedback with you, but I'm strapped for time to make it meaningful." (*But* = I choose me over Stacey.) Versus: "Stacey, I want to go over your feedback with you and I'm strapped for time to make it meaningful." (*And* = I want to choose you. My lack of time isn't helping).

* "Tanesha, I hear your suggestions, but I'm struggling to see how they'll work." (*But* = Tanesha's suggestions won't work, end of story). Versus: "Tanesha, I hear your suggestions and I'm struggling to see how they'll work." (*And* = Tanesha, help me see better how they will work.)

* "Luis, I know you won't have the proofs to me by Friday, but if I don't get them in time for the sales meeting then we're screwed." (*But* = it's your fault Luis.) Versus: "Luis, I know you won't have the proofs to me by Friday, and if I don't get them in time for the sales meeting, then we're screwed." (*And* = Luis, please help fix our problem).

* "My favorite cake flavor is mint chip ice cream cake, but if I had to choose one for everyone in the office to share, then I want chocolate." (*But* = disappointment that I didn't get mint chip). Versus: "My favorite birthday cake flavor is mint chip ice cream cake, and if I had to choose one for everyone in the office to share, then I want chocolate." (*And* = I like chocolate and we all get some.)

This replacement shift works. It disarms conflict and makes room for all thoughts, even ones that seem in opposition. It allows you to interact from a place of expansion and options rather than competition and either/or choices.

After drafting the rules of engagement, one of the delegates, who serves as treasurer, asked, "Did I hear correctly that we are not debating, today? If so, then what are we doing?"

CREATE A SHARED GOAL AND CONTEXT

We explained to them that our job today was to help them bridge the gap between their different perspectives so that they could effectively and meaningfully communicate and make decisions as a team. We reminded them of their shared goal: *Invest political action dollars strategically to solve problems and create positive impact in the industry.*

Let's pause and review the importance of a shared goal, especially in relationships where breakdowns have occurred. One way to bridge the gap is to consistently acknowledge and focus on the shared goal that exists in the relationship. When people struggle to show up clean or curious, a shared goal becomes the "North Star" to navigate your relationship by. It will keep you engaged and moving forward with them. Reminding the delegates of their shared goal and responsibility keeps them playing on the same team and focused.

After we reminded them of their shared goal, we introduced the bridge-the-gap graphic—which you've seen before, and here it is again: see Exhibit 6.1.

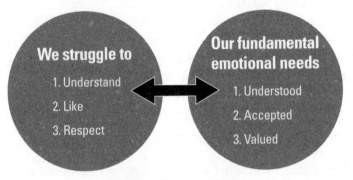

We struggle to

1. Understand

2. Like

3. Respect

Our fundamental emotional needs

1. Understood

2. Accepted

3. Valued

EXHIBIT 6.1 The Gap to Bridge

After we unpacked what that meant, we launched into a piece of our work-wife story about why we were hired to create context about why curiosity matters.

Jennifer began, "One of the reasons we were hired is because I'm a conservative and a Republican, and Katie is a liberal and a Democrat. In merging 45+ years of business, strategy, and knowledge, we've witnessed how easy it is for things to fall apart. This season we've just experienced—2020 to now—has been full of pressure, negativity, and polarization. We've witnessed the tightest of bonds break under the weight of miscommunication and arguments. We focus on our shared goal: helping people bridge the gap. Lowering our defenses to collaborate has been the gamechanger. We practice something called *curiosity over criticism*, when we want to growl, lash out, bite, and shred each other."

Katie continued, "Trust me, identifying as "blue" or "red" during 2020 has been tough. We totally get irritated, frustrated, annoyed, and sick of each other. We have different perspectives, values, and ways that we show up in defending and promoting our beliefs and opinions. This has been increasingly difficult to navigate because of external noise and pressure. It's been rough between the warring viewpoints of FOX and CNN and our friends and colleagues asking each of us:

> "Why are you working with a Republican? Is she a red hat? Be sure not to sell your soul—they are sneaky, exploitative, corrupt opportunists."

> "Why are you working with a Democrat? Is she a social-ist? Be sure not to give away your soul—they're sneaky, exploitative, corrupt opportunists."

"It's been difficult to walk the line, especially as we're lumped into labels and categories—when the reality is that when we explore our stories, beliefs, values, and more—we find various shades of purple rather than strict red and blue. When we lead with *curiosity over criticism*, it allows us to work through the breakdowns and create breakthroughs. It keeps our work alive."

Jennifer jumped in: "Please look at the graphic, again. How do you feel when your opinion, party, beliefs, and values are chal-lenged by someone who is opposite you? Do you feel understood, valued, or accepted? No. When anyone becomes locked into these 'debates,' emotional needs aren't met, and the relationship suf-fers, and our communication efforts stagnate and weaken. We speak and it falls flat or we speak and it creates a wildfire. So, this is what we wish for you—to stop playing the blame and shame game. Everyone is guilty of it, and it's time to stop if you really care about the industry, each other, this board, and the shared goal and outcome. We're not going to sugar coat it: bridging the gap requires you to communicate and collaborate with people who get under your skin. It requires stepping into the Explorer role and suspending—temporarily—what you think you know, what you were promised on the brochure, and you're sense of cer-tainty, being right, and 'winning.'"

"This is why you aren't engaging in a debate today," Katie added. "Nor will you have two-way conversations. A two-way conversation between heated opinions is a dynamic where nobody wins because you're both competing to be seen and heard from a place of ego, where you've been hijacked by strong emotions and beliefs."

SHIFTING TWO-WAY CONVERSATIONS TO CURIOUS ONE-WAY DIALOGUES

Let's pause and understand dynamics that derive from the structure of how we typically converse. It begins with how you grew up and learned to build most of your sentences. What's the formula? Start with a subject pronoun (I), add a verb and some adjectives and adverbs, maybe a prepositional phrase—and bam—you have a sentence and can join the conversation!

Many sentences and conversations are rooted in "I." This makes sense, because by nature, you are self-centered in your human suit, zipped into your own perspective (which you have crafted from the stories sitting in your filing cabinet in your limbic system).

We brought this awareness to the delegates to show them typical conversational dynamics that most people default to in their interactions and to further our point about having a debate. We used an easy, everyday example that wasn't hot and loaded. See if the following example echoes a mindless conversation you've experienced, too.

The Two-Way Conversation Dynamic

It's Monday morning and you're walking through the hallway to your desk. Coffee in hand, you smile and greet a few of your colleagues when one stops and warmly asks:

"Hey there! Good morning. How was your weekend?"

"Great! We went to the beach," you respond.

"I just don't get the sand thing. I'm a snow person—I love the mountains."

"Really?" you say. "I'd choose the waves over pine trees any day. Too cold for me."

"I just never got the appeal of sand—and it's always windy. Why is that?"

"I love the sun and sand—so relaxing—and the sound of the waves and . . ." You are about to finish your sentence when they interrupt.

"Well, I have this house up in Tahoe, and we go a lot during ski season. We drink hot chocolate, hang out at the fire pits, and bundle up. It's so much fun. Your family should come up with us sometime if you want to find out why the mountains are so awesome."

"Thanks! And same here—our beach spot is . . ."

This is a typical Monday morning conversation. And there's nothing wrong with it. These conversations are zippy, darting back and forth, me then you, my preferences over yours . . . like two drivers in the Daytona 500 race! Each person speeding and pulling out in front of the other, passing each other by as they aimlessly loop the tracks of small talk, using lots of "I"-centered language.

This conversation feels a bit like an energetic competition between two people. There isn't much curiosity, either. It's two people comparing and contrasting preferences with little depth and substance. And—for most of us—this is how we have been modeled to have conversations. You offer something. I make a counteroffer that shows how I relate and matter. You respond with a counter that shows how you relate and matter.

In conversations where you seek to better understand, like, or respect someone, volleying a conversation back and forth, where good communication looks like equal parts of talking and listening, is unsupportive. Leading with your "I" mucks up being curious.

Curious One-Way Dialogue Dynamic

Let's restructure this Daytona-style "one-upmanship" type of conversation into a more substantive dialogue, and this time you're the speaker who begins, leading with curiosity.

"Hey there! Good morning. How was your weekend?" you ask.

"It was great! We went to the beach."

"Ah, what beach?" you inquire, suspending your need to bring up that you aren't a beach person.

"Stinson: we love it there—if you head to the north side, you can let your dogs off leash."

"Cool. Tell me—did your dogs love it?" you ask, sipping your coffee.

"Oh! Yes! Our Chewy girl—we have only one dog—just loves the ocean. We recently adopted her and couldn't wait to take her to our favorite spot."

You latch onto the word "favorite," to lead your next question, curious about what that means to them. "What is special about that spot?"

"I dunno. Maybe it's because it's where my dogs have always gone with me, and since they've passed now, it's a place where I can reflect and be nostalgic. But at the same time Chewy makes it new and exciting again!"

"Water is always good for reflection. What are you most excited about in this fresh start?" you ask, again leading with their energy around the word they used: *exciting.*

"Calm. And a happy dog by my side."

"Sounds like you deserve that." You smile.

They reciprocate. "What about you, how was your weekend?"

See what shifted?

You, the questioner, stayed with the speaker and listened while posing open-ended, curious questions. Within seconds, the speaker dropped into specific details about their life, diving into their love of dogs. You, the smart cookie that you are, latched onto their words *favorite* and *exciting.* Both are subjective words that mean something to the speaker and in determining what that means for them, you learned a significant nugget—that the speaker is hoping for calm and joy.

That's connection, a small interaction that brings you closer together.

When the delegates read this dialogue out loud, we asked them to tell us what shifted, and if they noticed physical changes in their body as they read each passage. One of them said, "yes, there was no competition for both parties to get their point across." One said, "I felt more relaxed reading the latter story."

Whether the conversations you have are casual dialogues or strategic ones, the curious one-way approach naturally fosters better relationships. Leading with curiosity shows that you care about the other person, allowing them to open and connect.

FORMS OF CURIOSITY

After a brief break, we shared a screen on the platform with this statement:

> Curiosity is the antidote to polarization,
> stereotyping, and misunderstanding.

Katie began, "The truth is that to bridge the gap, you need to care. And it's hard to care about anyone's perspective when you don't understand or know them to a certain degree. This makes your job today, tough, right? Despite what you feel, the reality is you don't know each other, nor really what's happening in their world, their constituency, their region, their business. Curiosity is the path to knowing them, to caring."

"Let's explore curiosity," Jennifer said, "because you all were born with copious amounts, and its replenishable, so let's use up this natural resource."

Curiosity is a natural, biological driver of behavior that is stitched into our human suits. Everyone is born curious. Embedded within our core is a desire to feel, experience, learn, and know the people and stuff that populates our slice of life.

There is a science to curiosity, and neuroscientists and researchers from Stanford, UC Berkeley, and beyond are learning how to "operationalize" curiosity—that is, putting curiosity into action to improve the workplace and people's lives. The research shows that adults engage in three types of curiosity on a regular basis:

- *Diversive Curiosity* happens when you're bored: *I need something to energize this rebranding effort. I feel so blah about the direction we're headed. Let me go see what Bill is doing in product design. I'm always inspired by his ingenuity and creativity.*

- **Epistemic Curiosity** is about your love of learning: *Social psychology and organizational dynamics is totally my jam. I'm such a nerd and can't wait to read this book called* Bridge the Gap *to expand my knowledge.*
- **Specific Curiosity** is about your desire to master an activity: *I've always wanted to teach karate, but they won't hire me if I'm not a black belt. I'm going to earn that color by participating in everything I can and will get my butt kicked until I dominate.*

Then there is the fourth type of curiosity, and this is the one we want to operationalize in how we communicate and collaborate, especially in diverse work environments and at the delegates' workshop:

- **Perceptual Curiosity** is something you activate when something captures your attention. It happens when you encounter something, or someone, you don't understand. At work, it often shows up when you are stuck inside a problem and can't figure out what to do: *I don't get what's going on with Melanie in HR, how come she won't answer my emails? Can someone please shed some light for me because what the heck, Melanie?!?!*

Research shows that throughout our lives, people engage in diverse, epistemic, and specific curiosity on a regular basis. The issue is that as we age, our perceptual curiosity takes a nosedive and plummets. Instead of seeking to bridge the gap between our perceptions and what's happening, our hijacked Inner Narrator feeds us stories, we dig into our biases, and we stop communicating across the gap.

For instance, in the example above, when your perceptual curiosity is lying somewhat dormant, you might assume that the problem lies wholly with Melanie. Your hijacked Inner Narrator will convince you that she is horrible at her job in HR and that you need to jump the chain of command to bypass her to get answers.

In your impatience, you lose curiosity about Melanie. This behavior impacts your relationship, no matter how deep or what kind of relationship you had with her.

Whereas a person leading with curiosity asks, "I wonder why Melanie hasn't answered my emails yet? I'm getting nervous *and* I should probably give her the benefit of the doubt. I'll go connect with her to see what's going on."

Intentionally weaving perceptual curiosity into our communication strategies and skills can save a lot of suffering, heartache, and unnecessary anger and frustration. You can improve the quality of your communication by leading with curiosity, instead of jumping to criticism and assumptions . . . and by letting go of any emotionally-driven need you have to change the other person—or group.

After working through this with the delegation, Jennifer interjected, "Hmm. Sounds too good to be true. Curiosity can also be used as a weapon, right? He who gets to be curious holds great power. . . !"

"Ah, yes, thanks Jennifer for being a voice of truth. When does our curiosity turn into fraud?" Katie asked the team.

CURIOSITY FRAUD

Now, let's "flip the script" and view the slippery slope of perceptual curiosity and when it becomes curiosity fraud, using the Melanie HR example:

- Curiosity turns fraudulent when your questions are bait and you're fishing for a particular response or reaction to fit your endgame: "Melanie, how many emails do you get a day? Seems like mine fall to the bottom! How do you decide who not to ignore? What do I have to do around here to make the cut?"
- Curiosity turns fraudulent when your agenda or emotional need to be understood, valued, accepted, and "right" colors the entire conversation. "Melanie, how come you never respond to my emails—what am I chopped liver? I thought you liked me."

- Curiosity turns fraudulent when questions are posed in a way that diminishes the experience, identity, or perspective of the other person. "You must have an overwhelming job, right? How do you manage, given that I read somewhere that millennials struggle with email and workplace communication, in general?"
- Curiosity turns fraudulent when someone cajoles, pressures, or demands an answer while claiming that he or she is "just being curious. "What's your work schedule like today? 'Cause I'm just curious about when you will respond to my email. . . ."
- Curiosity turns fraudulent with incessant whys that are aimed to sting or shame. "Why is your response time three days? Why didn't you see the email?"

Several people snickered at the healthcare event when we had them read these examples out loud. Each person spoke with a tone that implied they had experienced curiosity fraud before. We heard voices sprinkled with fake sugar, snark, apathy, directness, and whine.

We all agreed that tone makes a huge difference in how we communicate. We agreed to not commit curiosity fraud.

SHOW UP CLEAN, CURIOUS, AND WITH CARE

We wrapped up the morning with the delegation having finalized the rules of engagement: be perceptually curious, replace *but* with *and,* don't fall into the two-way dynamic, and choose to care. We prepared them for the rest of the experience, surprising them with a twist:

"Now, we'll have a working lunch over the course of two hours. You'll be placed in breakout rooms, and your team lead will help you draft stories about what it means to identify within your politics, how it impacts your voice and vote, and the values you're representing within your constituency. Katie will take the red team—the more conservative, Republican-identifying party, and Jennifer will take the blue team—the more liberal, Democratic-identifying party."

"Jennifer, I can't wait to hear the stories of the red team! I love being blue in a sea of red," Katie cheered.

"Ditto." Jennifer waved to the team and let them go for a fifteen-minute break.*

We leave this chapter with one final thought: when people are stuck in the finger trap, they often feel like they don't have a choice about how to behave differently. We believe that when you show up clean, curious, and with care (see Exhibit 6.2) . . . you enter a choice paradigm—where you can respond versus react and show up differently to bridge the gap.

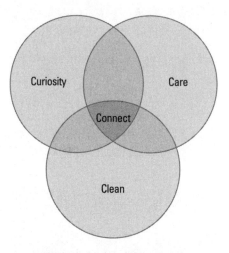

EXHIBIT 6.2 The Art of Connection

Showing up curious is really about suspending yourself: emotions, lived experiences, identity labels, and knowledge. It's about opening up and listening to the perspective, lived experiences, and values of another. It's a tall order and not easy. In the next chapter, you will dive into how you listen and tools to overcome biased listening to show up curious and begin bridging the gap.

---

* Rest assured, in Chapter 9, you will return to the delegation to see what transpired.

REFLECTION QUESTIONS

- Think about the best conversation you have ever had, one where you felt seen, heard, understood. What contributed to that conversational structure that made you feel the above? What was the flow?
- Where might you explore replacing *and* over *but*?
- Identify a Daytona raceway conversation you have recently had. What was the energy and experience like for you? How do you think it was for the other person?

ACTION ITEM
The Choice: One-Way Over Two-Way

Choose to have a curious one-way dialogue with someone that you're usually in a two-way Daytona conversation with at work. Afterward, reflect on how that conversation made you feel, how the other person felt, and if you learned anything that could help you connect—and care—more about them.

JOIN THE CONVERSATION
#andoverbut

CLEAN AND CURIOUS LISTENING
Hurdles and Headphones

Think about the incessant distractions that pressure people to react. Messages vie for your attention everywhere—noise bellowing at you from television, social media, a fervent news cycle, clickbait headlines. . . ! At work, you also manage distractions from your personal life, along with other noise: staffing issues, reluctant clients, balance sheet concerns, a slog of emails to address. . . !

Most of us are stuck in a maddening and overwhelming swirl of daily noise and pressure. And your reliable frenemy AMY and your Inner Narrator tend to shove you into a reactive state as you filter incoming pressure, often judging the noise before you can pause and hear what's being actually said, offered, or asked of you. Remember that your executive function, when under pressure, can be hijacked for up to 26 hours. In this crazy world of juggling roles and responsibilities, it can be tough to know:

- What to believe . . .
- Who to trust . . .
- What is important . . .
- How to respond . . .

Let's enhance your current listening skills to cut through the noise to gain clarity and connect and communicate beyond surface-level distractions. To bridge the gap, you will need clean and curious listening skills, but first there are some hurdles to be aware of and some adjustments to make on a pair of invisible headphones that you unconsciously wear.

YOUR HURDLES TO LISTENING

Let's start using our two ears and one mouth in proportion.

Often, too much emphasis is placed on language to do the hard work of communication. Words often fail us. Have you ever found yourself intently listening to someone and then realized that you're no longer listening, but have fallen down a rabbit hole of your own thinking? These days, many of us are impatient in our listening because our attention spans have diminished. In fact, *Time* magazine ran an article with the intriguing title, "You Now Have a Shorter Attention Span Than a Goldfish," based on research by Microsoft, that found our attention spans have dropped from twelve seconds to eight seconds.[1] These distractions of the mind are natural, especially in our fast-paced technological world where we've been conditioned to quickly access stories, information, and content to make snap decisions in our human suits.

We call these distractions "hurdles" because they will always exist on the path of listening. Like the Drama Triangle, there are default behaviors that we tend to slide into when it comes to being present and listening well. We have identified four main "hurdles" that we must jump over if we want to truly hear something of value and connect. See if you, your team, and/or a colleague are lagging at one, some, or all the hurdles.

The Impatience Hurdle

James is a junior salesman in the solar industry and on a mission to save the planet. Up at dawn and ready to go, he is scrappy and ambitious, taking on the challenge to convince people to go green. Paid on commission, he is driving and grinding day in and day out. His favorite expression is: "Watch out! I am coming in hot!"

Somehow, this approach isn't working. His close rate is the lowest on the team, and his paycheck has the proof.

The head of sales called us in to spend a day with James. First, James proudly showed us how many meetings he had stacked up in one day. While watching him work with a prospect, we immediately noticed the Impatience Hurdle (see Exhibit 7.1).

ONE

- Formulating a response while another speaks
- Toe-tapping: believing that we know what they're going to say
- Jumping in without letting them complete their thought or fully processing it
- Sighing, looking around, and saying "yep, yep, yep"

EXHIBIT 7.1 The Impatience Hurdle

James comes on with a fury when with potential buyers— he thinks high energy and rambunctious passion equals sales. Throughout the "conversation," he pitched relentlessly. He didn't listen, nor did he express curiosity about any questions that the prospect might have. Nor did he spend time transforming his love for green solar into meaningful stories about the cost-saving value of solar energy and its impact on the environment. He pushed the "conversation" (which was not a conversation) forward by talking fast, predicting questions, and then answering his own questions to appear smart and clever. Sometimes we wondered if he was performing a one-man theater show. The prospect felt pressured and looked at us several times to save them. It was painful to not jump in and save James. His energy is frenetic and impatient, as if telling the prospect, "Come on . . . this is stupid easy . . . just buy already."

They didn't.

At the end of the day, we asked him if it was normal to close zero sales with so many lined up.

He said, "Yes! You just must find the right buyer at the right moment. It's sales 101."

We bit our tongues at that deflection of responsibility. With that response, we could see that he had convinced himself that the prospects weren't ready—for solar, for him. In further coaching sessions, we showed him the Impatience Hurdle graphic. We asked him if he was guilty of any of those behaviors. James is a smart guy—just a bit full of himself. You can tell that he wants to be good at his job, earn money, help the environment, and win sales awards.

He laughed. "Of course! Who isn't?"

Again, his deflection of *This is normal, not just me*, was very interesting . . . and we were glad that he had no shame or personal feelings about being shown how his lack of listening and communicating well were keeping him from sizable paychecks. Then we asked him if it might be possible to show up differently in his next meeting and resist acting "drunk on his own passion for green energy." We asked him to slow down, listen, and be fully present with his prospects. We rehearsed with role-modeling activities.

He didn't close any deals on his first, second, or third conversations. However, the fourth was a winner. He said that by being aware of how he was listening and speaking, he was able to jump the hurdle and connect better. By embracing a new approach, his conversion percentage shot through the roof.

The Preoccupied Hurdle

All of us struggle to be present because as adults, we are often preoccupied with many things listed in Exhibit 7.2.

One of our clients, a woman who owns an art gallery and artists' cooperative in beautiful Carmel, California, came to us sobbing. She acknowledged that she had been snooping at home and came across her daughter's journal and dove in. The entries broke her heart and one woke her up: "It is like my mom isn't even here anymore. She pretends but isn't. I can't stand how she is always posting on Facebook and Instagram these pics of us being a family when really, we don't even talk that much. I mean really, mom, you tell me not to numb and scroll and play pretend, but

TWO

- Your phone or wearable technology
- To-do lists that vie for your attention
- Scrolling mindlessly on social media and news
- Background noise: television, radio, others' talking
- Distracted by shiny objects
- A crisis/hurt feeling that you are currently enduring

EXHIBIT 7.2 The Preoccupied Hurdle

where do you think I learned it? All you do is scroll and look at your phone."

Oofta. This story hits close to home for many of us working and busy parents and caregivers.

We told her that this moment was a mirror and a window. She was able to see herself clearly reflected in her daughter's journal. She concurred that indeed she always felt "elsewhere" instead of just inside the moment. She admitted that her social media life didn't exactly portray reality. Then we asked her to stop looking in the mirror and see through the window of possibility of what might happen to her relationship with her daughter—and others—if she became more present when with others.

She committed to putting away all distractions and clearing her mind to be in the moment and conversation with others. Not only did her relationship with her daughter change, but her business model also ended up changing for the better. Working with creatives and artists can be challenging—it takes a special person to broker art into sales. It's a difficult industry between pricing and curating art, finding collectors, and launching unknown artists who are fresh and relevant. She knew that anyone who purchases a piece of art that costs thousands of dollars is not only buying the piece itself but the artist's story behind the piece, too.

In showing up present with her artists, she heard more deeply the stories of why they created a certain piece and how their aesthetic and medium contributed to its meaning. This jostled her, just like her daughter's journal. She had no idea the depth inside the people around her because she was living elsewhere. To that end, she pivoted how she sold online. Instead of creating quippy posts and graphics to sell and promote the art on social media, she began videotaping how her artists spoke about their work—with such presence, hope, heart, and meaning—and when she posted those videos online, buyers came. Showing up clean and curious in her listening made a huge difference.

The Selfish Hurdle

Let's be honest, we are hardwired for selfishness; it's part of being zipped into a human suit. Being selfish means we are meeting our own needs to feel safe, understood, valued, and accepted. And that's great for setting boundaries, practicing self-care, and tending to ourselves as whole humans. At work, though, strong personalities tend to get stuck at this hurdle because they struggle to not dominate teamwork and work as a collaborator. Exhibit 7.3 illustrates.

THREE

- Shifting the conversation to make it about you
- Focusing on our ego and needs
- Jumping to self-righteousness before hearing all the information
- Falling down the rabbit hole of our own stories
- Stewing in judgement, criticism, and annoyance when the other speaks

EXHIBIT 7.3 The Selfish Hurdle

It's always about them.

Remember Claire (from Chapter 2)? The executive director from the theater who wanted to blow up at her board and show them who is really in charge? Well, the situation worsened. She didn't send the email—but continued to lambaste her board for how they weren't "performing for her." In spending lots of time with Claire (because we love her despite her feisty selfishness), we were able to count how many times in a single conversation she made it about herself—and not the mission of her theater company. With gentleness, we asked her to look at the Selfish Hurdle and identify some things she may have been guilty of, especially within the dynamics of her relationship with the board as a whole and, also, at the individual level with each board member.

At first, she resisted.

Then we asked her if there were times when she was out promoting the theater company or if those presentations were just about promoting herself—her stories, talents, strengths, and background as an award-winning stage actress from New York.

"I know what attracts people and if I'm being honest, it often is me." She said, kind of smugly.

Oh, Claire.

"Hmm, I didn't peg you as an arrogant person," Katie pushed. "I thought this was a mission-driven organization with lots of volunteers, community support, patrons, and a board of amazing leaders pitching in to make the theater the best company in the region. Am I wrong?"

Claire fell silent and narrowed her eyes at Katie.

Jennifer put her hand on Claire's shoulder. "I know that was probably hard to hear. While a leader might be the channel for the work, for achieving the vision . . . it's not about you. It's a team effort, and every time you show up to perform 'the Claire show,' you're leaving people behind. You're not allowing them to participate, give, and belong to something bigger."

That did it. Claire pled guilty to all her crimes. She admitted she has been a lone wolf most of her life and has figured out ways to use her charm to be successful. We told her she wasn't a lone wolf anymore: she had a pack to inspire, empower, and lead. We assured her she wouldn't lose any of her magic by shifting the spotlight to others—it would only enhance it.

We coached her to transform her stories—the arsenal of content she had built up to attract and keep people's attention—to show up differently and engage others in the magic. She began meeting her board, donors, and staff with curiosity about why they gave time, talent, and treasure to the theater. She intentionally didn't front-load the interactions with anything personal about her. She even went on a listening tour to hear about what the community at large hoped the theater could do, be, and achieve. In, the end, she learned to be part of a team and communicate better as a leader.

The "I Just Can't Help Myself" Hurdle

Do you know someone who dominates conversations? Fills space with noise? Doesn't even give five seconds for someone to respond before moving to the next topic? See Exhibit 7.4 for other aspects of this hurdle.

FOUR

- Filling the space with noise because silence feels uncomfortable
- Answering questions and offering advice
- Looking smart and showing off
- Being more interesting than interested
- Solving problems without empowering the speaker to do it on their own
- Conflating our experiences with theirs and interrupting with "me, too" stories

EXHIBIT 7.4 The "I Just Can't Help Myself" Hurdle

At coffee one day, a client-turned-friend shared a story that we asked her to write in a letter to you (our readers) to illustrate the power of this hurdle and what you might miss out on if you keep filling the space with your speech:

Dear Reader,

They say that silence is golden. Silence can also be incredibly painful. Sometimes two minutes of silence with a stranger can feel like a lifetime! Sitting across the table, waiting in baited anticipation, locked in an awkward staring contest with the human on the other side of the table. Slow blinking. Breathing . . . in and out and hearing every last molecule of air exit from their lungs. . . . Listening to the "tick, tick" of your watch as several empty seconds pass by that feel like a hollow forever. And then you can't take it anymore, and you burst wide open to fill the blank space. With something. Anything!! Anything that will take away that painful, awkward silence.

We generally all want to connect. This means that interactions with other extroverted people are really natural. Either they do all the talking and then make a decision about us, or we compete for the floor and hopefully in the process find some common ground and decide we like each other. When we are interacting with others who are a bit slower to respond and pause to think, we can find ourselves in the muck.

I am a hiring professional and business growth consultant. I help companies identify candidates for hire, which means I conduct a lot of interviews every year. Which means I sit across the table (or computer screen) from hundreds of other people (a.k.a. "strangers") every year and participate in a process that aims to dive below the surface and into real authenticity very quickly in order to make a very big life decision . . . and in a matter of a few hours. (That seems fair and totally reasonable, right?)

Truth: Interviews favor the extroverted talker. Those with the "gift of gab."

Now, I am someone who processes information very quickly, with words zinging through my head and flopping out my mouth sometimes faster than logic can keep up with. This is common for certain types of people—sales professionals, executives, and the like. That said, there are some folks who walk among us in the world who prefer to swallow in information with their oxygen, think deeply, and then provide an (often more well-thought-out and less flopped) response. They can't help themselves. Some people think before they speak. This is good news for the world! And bad news in an interview.

A common pattern I often observe among interviewers is to feel that silence is painful, and to fill blank space with words, questions and small talk. And what happens?

I often observe candidates who do not have an opportunity to speak much during the interview, dominated by a brash hiring manager who is perhaps in a hurry just to get to the bottom line, more motivated by the clock than by true connection. The debrief goes something like this:

"What did you think of Curtis?"

"Well, he barely said anything, so it's hard to say. I didn't really connect with him."

"THAT'S BECAUSE YOU NEVER LET HIM TALK!"

"Curtis wasn't saying a whole lot, so I felt I needed to keep the conversation moving."

"It's okay to have blank space. Silence over speaking."

What happens when we don't give others the space to share? We fail to connect truly and authentically. We also fill in the gaps with our own assumptions. We never actually get to their true need because we falsely anticipate it, and thus, we sometimes find our foot firmly inserted into our mouth. When we don't get to know someone and adequately build that critical relationship, we don't land the deal. We make a bad hire. We don't make new friends.

Our natural tendency is to want to fill that empty space because it feels uncomfortable and we can't help ourselves.

The next time you are in an interview, ask a question. And then sit. In blank space. No matter how weird it feels to sit and watch the other person's face, I promise, eventually that person will talk. Let them. And then ask again. Keep going layer after layer into the question until you have reached authenticity. They will feel heard. You will have the answer. And you will both win.

There is real power in harnessing that quiet and blank space. Silence over speaking.

With you,

Katie McConnell Olson

Founder & CEO, Hire Education Consulting Group, Inc.

Katie McConnell Olson speaks powerfully to the value of silence—allowing people to process and think before responding.

We've spent a lot of time in classrooms around the nation, and one difference we notice between great teachers and okay ones is the value they place on silence and the rules they impose about silence. Great teachers pose a question and then provide space before allowing anyone (not that kid in the front row, itching to jump out of their chair with their hand raised) to respond. Great teachers give around eight seconds of silence before calling on someone to answer. This magic number (which you'll learn about later) is a difference maker in the quality of responses and learning that can happen for everyone (not just the A-types, extroverts, and eager beavers with their hands raised high). Great teachers, like great communicators, are comfortable with silence—offering space for others to speak.

Quality listening is tough for anyone, and it takes practice. The biology disruption techniques from Chapter 5 are immensely helpful to activate if you want to be a great listener. The four hurdles we've just described are barriers in nearly all your conversations. Before we give you a tool to employ, ask yourself: Which hurdles consistently appear before you? Which ones are you "jumping over" to show up clean and curious in your listening?

When anyone struggles to jump over the hurdles, we encourage them to slow down their thoughts internally, gain spaciousness, and try to let go of the noise and distractions. This awareness will allow you to better bridge gaps. When listening becomes difficult, focus on your breathing. You can listen and breathe at the same time! With each inhalation and exhalation, your brain's prefrontal cortex generates clarity, curiosity, and presence. The more oxygen you can feed your brain by breathing through your nose, the greater you can focus.[2]

Now that you've identified the hurdles on the path to listening, let's address how you filter what you hear when someone speaks.

YOU ARE WEARING A PAIR OF HEADPHONES

When we were young girls, we got our first Walkmans and were introduced to headphones. What a novelty back then! Our parents would try to get our attention, but we were grooving to Madonna and The Cure and that noise was all we could hear. We could turn the volume waaaay up to drown out the world, especially our parents. Or we could turn the music down and play it softly so that we could still be with them, but while listening to our tunes.

At work and in our daily interactions, you wear invisible headphones that filter how you hear and interpret information. How well you listen with these headphones impacts how you process the people, noise, messages, distractions, and environment around us. And your headphones can change dramatically or subtly depending on your awareness level, mood, emotional and physical needs in that moment, how you want to be perceived, and your listening hurdles.

➤ The Big Aha! ◄

What is most interesting, however, is that most of us rarely consider that we wear any kind of headphones at all. We roll through our workday and life on autopilot, not considering that our headphones are filtering what people say, ask, and want of us. Chances are you may be guilty of listening in "sloppy" ways because your headphones constrict you from "clean" listening where you can be curious and open to hear what's really coming at you.

SLOPPY LISTENING

Sloppy listening damages communication and relationships and impedes collaboration.

Let's explore three ways that sloppy listening shows up and ruins the music that can be made between you and others.

1. Suspicious, Defensive Listening

"Why do you think that?"

"Where did you come up with that idea?"

"Who told you that?"

"Oh, yeah? Keep trying to convince me."

Remember Michael, the men's fashion expert, from Chapter 4? While working with him, we noticed something else about his approach that led to his eventual exit. His headphones filtered most messages and interactions with various levels of suspicion, and it ultimately made him guarded and defensive. Michael was often leery about certain words, pieces of information, harmless nods and/or smiles, and the way that people looked at him. As we saw with Trent and the bow ties, he was defensive about various perspectives, ideas, or opinions. Admittedly, when we met him, he was not in a great space—but that only served to amplify his level of defensiveness and suspicious listening. And since he resisted being even a little psychologically flexible, he further trapped himself into a listening pattern that also contributed to his firing.

Suspicious, defensive listening has a tone beyond just being inquisitive or adding to the discussion your knowledge, concerns, or questions. In extreme cases like Michael's, this listening filter brings obstinance and blockages into our relationships. Of course, we all desire flow and ease in how we volley thoughts and ideas back and forth with someone. We want to be comfortable enough to challenge our colleagues if we aren't completely sold. Suspicious, defensive listening doesn't work though because it disrespects the speaker and fails to meet their fundamental emotional needs. It creates distance instead of bridging the gap.

At its root, this type of listening filters much of what's being said with fear and resistance. Often, people with this listening pattern forget to assume that most of their colleagues come to conversations with positive intent—but these listeners don't really believe the speaker knows what they're talking about, which damages trust and respect.

Of course, neither the soured Inner Narrator nor Michael sees it this way. They have built many stories in their mind and in the filing cabinets of their limbic system about why they challenge and ask questions. They struggle to hear any negative tone in their voice (that's the immense power of these invisible headphones). It's easy for them to find experiences in the past where their suspicious, defensive listening worked on their behalf. They use evidence from the past to justify their current behavior—even though it's a new day, a new team, a new idea, a new opportunity. AMY, their soured Inner Narrator, and past stories drag them down.

On the less extreme side, suspicious, defensive listening can show up as:

- *Bitter sarcasm:* "Seriously? Aren't you Captain Smarty Pants with all that knowledge from podcasts!?!?"
- *Dismissiveness:* "I used to be that optimistic, too. Call me in a few years when you figure it out. There's really nothing new."
- *"Friendly" Debate:* "OK. Let me play devil's advocate, did you consider the news report this morning about how apples really are healthier for you than oranges?"

It's a listening pattern that loves to challenge what the other thinks or proposes. It positions the listener as someone who needs convincing, and that dynamic alone quickly breeds hostility, hampering the level of trust and respect in relationships. This listening never bridges gaps; in fact, it widens them.

Who likes to work with someone who needs convincing all the time?

Nobody.

2. Passive, Pleaser Listening

"Yep."

"Ok."

"Mm-hmm."

Ever been in a conversation with someone who "yeps" you to death as you're speaking, and it becomes clear that they aren't really listening? There is a difference between someone agreeing versus mindlessly agreeing. Our next sloppy listening filter is *passive, pleaser listening*, and it's rampant and quite understandable.

There are many times when we hear information and feel awkward, unclear, insecure, or perhaps even thrown by what's being said. Instead of becoming suspicious or defensive, we choose to be passive. We mindlessly agree with what the speaker is saying to appease them. We avoid asking questions and don't participate in the conversation with our own thoughts or counterresponses. For example, this filter shows up often in heated topics like politics and really in any place where conflict might arise.

You know it's passive, pleaser listening when the listener's energy lacks engagement. Also, we added "pleaser" to this listening filter because this filter is essentially about avoiding discomfort, which *pleases* both the listener and the speaker because there is no potential for dissension or debate. And it makes sense because people whose headphones filter information with this filter are often at a loss of how to show up and engage in the conversation. Listeners with this filter often fear offending, misspeaking, or falling into a debate with the speaker. In addition, many people default to this listening mode because they simply don't care or have the energy or time necessary to fully respond. It's often easier to let the speaker carry on with their thoughts, stories, and opinions. We succumb to a series of *ok*, *mm-hmm*, and *yep* as we "listen."

There's a clear difference between listening to learn with curiosity to bridge the gap, and listening in a passive, pleaser position.

Our friend Arlene—bless her heart—is a classic passive, pleaser listener. She is a "platinum-level director" in a multi-level marketing company where she sells jewelry and accessories to modern professional women. She sells directly to her own clients while also leading a team of sixty-five sales representatives. She still throws old-school jewelry trunk show parties at people's houses on weekends and evenings—so you can imagine the spectrum of people she meets in their homes and the stories they share with her as she sets up her goods to sell.

Arlene is also one of the most well-read women we know. She stays up on current events, reads news from a plethora of sources, is a critical thinker, and has opinions. At her parties, it makes sense that she stays neutral—pleasing the clients, listening to their opinions and stories while being a guest in their homes. However, when it comes to motivating and training her team—her passive, pleaser listening filter gets her trouble.

Given the nature of her working a home-based business, she coaches many mothers and eager young women who are trying to build more wealth. The personal and professional are always intermingling. You can imagine that the COVID-19 pandemic, a divisive election, and more, have impacted how her team shows up and engages with each other. When her team veers into conversations that get heated, she rarely steps up as the leader to shift the team's energy to more productive topics.

She checks out.

She fails to listen to what's being said and to shut down polarizing discussions, which can turn off many members in her team. When we asked her why she was showing up this way, she said she doesn't ever want to interrupt someone. She's simply too polite, too nervous. So, you can imagine that when nine women on her team branched off to start their own training program and stopped coming to hers, she was devastated. And these nine women were crucial motivators and role models to the rest of the women. When she was brave enough to ask them about their decision to splinter off, they responded with, "We never felt supported or heard when we expressed our opinions or concerns." In a paradoxical moment, Arlene was flummoxed because she always let them carry on with their opinions and concerns. Arlene's lack of engagement and passivity backfired because . . . she wasn't listening.

Who likes to work with a checked-out person, a passive pleaser? Nobody.

3. Biased Listening

"I know. I work in this field. I am an expert."

"Look, I grew up in this industry—you are not telling me anything I don't already know."

"Well, what you don't understand is . . ."

"What you're forgetting is . . ."

Here's an obvious truth bomb: *All humans are biased.*

There is not a single person alive who isn't biased. The Dalai Lama, the Pope, the yogi down at the meditation studio . . . all biased in their ways of being and thinking. Everyone, to some degree, wears biased headphones. We are often unconscious of our deeply entrenched biases. We become blind and deaf to how we show up, communicate, connect, and collaborate.

The danger comes when we can't suspend our knowledge, experiences, or way of being to hear a new or diverse perspective.

Our identity exists at the intersection of our biology and our lived experiences. Based on our culture, values, experiences, files in the limbic system, AMY, and our Inner Narrator, we all make judgments and derive meaning from our biases. Just like we can't zip off our human suit, we can't easily zip off our biases. It's a long process of growing personal awareness and taking responsibility to change our behaviors and thoughts to reshape neural wiring to address bias—especially toxic biases that are discriminatory (racism, sexism, etc.).

This type of sloppy listening is utterly uninterested in the phrase *you don't know what you don't know.* In *biased listening,* our Inner Narrator seeks to hear things that confirm our identity— our perspectives, lived experiences, expectations, and stories. With this filter, we often interject our expertise, stories, experiences, and more to control the conversation. This can lead to distortion and a willingness to only hear information one singular "right" way.

Professor Stuart is a genius. Distinguished honors and awards, loads of publications—he is an expert in the field of political science and history. For him, everything boils down to military history and various American presidencies. It's nearly impossible to have a conversation with him without him pointing to a time in history where a general, military crew, or war faced a similar problem. It's like his entire lens for viewing the world is skewed through his knowledge.

Professor Stuart does not live in a vacuum; he is paid to do a job like every other worker in the nation. He works on a campus with many other brilliant minds and thousands of students from diverse backgrounds. While great at giving lectures and writing dissertations, he sucks at being with people, especially in important committee work at the university. One of his biases that shows up—which we think he's unconscious of—is that he coats everything in masculine terms and energy. Every metaphor, analogy, and example are male-driven. It's like women don't exist. And when confronted about it, he has several stories queued up with, "Well, what you don't understand is that women . . . blah blah blah blah blah blah blah blah blah blah."

We taught a daylong workshop on campus about the listening filters, and several female professors in our work groups mentioned Professor Stuart as an example. They pointed to how he struggles to include various perspectives or intersect his expertise with other fields of academia and therefore can't collaborate or function in his committee work. Nobody wants to work with him, no matter how brilliant and knowledgeable he might be. His bias against women is shooting him in the foot because he can't listen to others and hear how he shows up in conversations outside the classroom. This listening never bridges gaps; in fact, it widens them.

Who likes to work with a know-it-all, unconscious of their biases?

Nobody.

AN ELEVATED CHOICE—
CLEAN, CURIOUS LISTENING

The hurdles and headphone filters are intense. Anyone who wants to connect, communicate, and collaborate better at work has their job cut out for them!

It's likely that your headphones impede some of your ability to truly listen, making you guilty of some or all the sloppy listening filters. The key is to be aware. For example, ask yourself these questions: When your listening turns sloppy . . .

1. Who are you with? How does that person trigger your AMY or the Inner Narrator?
2. What hurdle(s) limit your listening?
3. How is your Inner Narrator keeping you from hearing others, and can you shush it?
4. How is it serving your efforts to communicate and get along better?
5. Are you able to adjust your headphones and cut out the noise and pressure to listen differently?

Let's give you a way to adjust your headphones that might be "preset" on one of the sloppy listening filters. With practice, you can shift and adjust the volume toward *clean listening*. It's a conscious-based skill that is both aspirational and achievable.

Just like "clean eating," *clean, curious listening* takes practice because it's not in our natural state to do what's good or "right" for us and change core behaviors. Like being addicted to sugar, you are easily addicted to sloppy listening because it gives you a free pass to continue with your listening patterns and behaviors.

When we must do the uncomfortable job of coaching folks like Michael, Arlene, Professor Stuart, and Claire to see how their sloppy listening and inner narration is messing up their ability to connect and communicate better—they first come with a suitcase of excuses.

"This is just who I am, I guess."

"Can't teach an old dog new tricks."

"I'm just trying to be nice—they don't care what I think anyway."

"I am an expert and know things. They should respect that and welcome my questions and thoughts."

"I'm not biased. My lived experiences prove that. . . ."

Some of those statements are canyons. Some are gaps. We ask for a commitment to try something new in service of having better relationships at work. We suggest clean, curious listening, which looks like this:

- Listen with your full attention. Be present and put away your technology and distractions. Consciously invite your Inner Narrator to take a nap.
- Be honest about your biases if you're aware of them and check them at the door.
- Forget what you know when you're listening. Ideas, thoughts, and your expertise or knowledge can come out later.
- Suspend judgments and assumptions.
- Engage your perceptual curiosity to learn more about the speaker.
- No need to fix anything; listen to keep gathering information until the time comes to collaborate with them on a solution.
- Bring patience. Don't rush the speaker or conversation.
- Allow for silence.
- Let the person in front of you finish complete thoughts and stories. Don't interrupt their thought processes with yours. Don't anticipate what they are going to say and show off by interrupting to show that you know where they are headed. There is no need to compete with your own story, or "one-up" theirs.
- Listen for what is being said underneath the words being used. Watch for when their face crumples with negative energy or lights up with positive energy. Look at their body language.
- Engage—show them that you're listening (nod, smile, make soft eye contact, lean gently in).

Clean, curious listening is being in a state of pure curiosity with a clear mind to be fully with the speaker. Biologically speaking, the experience of being in a conversation where clean, curious listening is enacted provides safety and respect to the speaker. It engages their prefrontal cortex and often fulfills their fundamental emotional needs. Under these conditions, people "magically" engage, and this encourages reciprocity, which helps your work and relationship flourish.

And if all else fails, remember this adage:

> Surely it is no coincidence that the word "listen"
> is an anagram of the word "silent."

Or just shut up the chatter internally and externally and listen—that works, too.

REFLECTION QUESTIONS

- Identify your hurdles and watch them play out during your day. When did they show up and how did you maneuver around them?
- When you are under pressure, what is filtered through your headphones? Is there a pattern that you're aware of when it shows up?
- When you are at ease, what happens to your listening?
- Are there moments when clean, curious listening comes naturally? Is there a way for you to summon it or invite it in during critical interactions?

ACTION ITEM
The Choice: Clean over Sloppy

As you prepare for your work week, choose one or two upcoming engagements and think through how you will be aware of your listening hurdles. Go into that engagement with an intentional focus and clean listening headphones.

JOIN THE CONVERSATION AND INTERACT ONLINE
#cleanlistening

TRUST AND RESPECT
Tending to Your Shared Egg

They didn't seem to like each other very much, if at all.

As for trust and respecting one another? What had been a promising partnership between two brilliant minds—where iron could sharpen iron—was quickly becoming a war of iron fighting iron.

As C-suite peers at a global bank, George, the chief information officer, and Tom, the chief financial officer, held positions that required them to work seamlessly together as they led enormous departments within a corporation that employed thousands of people.

George and Tom were both "commercially raised" in their careers, but in wildly different Fortune 50 companies. Both executives were highly valued, beyond ambitious, technically skilled, and overall, talented hard workers. But each came to their positions with different experiences about how success and achievement were defined. Each engaged their staff differently, leading and communicating as previously defined by their former Fortune 50 cultures. In executive cabinet meetings, the strain between them was palpable.

George was a connector—gregarious, verbose, and wicked smart at IT strategy and cybersecurity. George's nickname at the bank was "The Translator," because of how he was able to help everyone, including the board, understand IT issues using plain, everyday language. George's true talent was the ability to transform complexity into simplicity. On the flipside, George was also known as someone who talks too much. His love of people meant that he spent probably *too* much time inside other peoples' stories and, of course, telling his own. While beloved by many, George had the potential to rub people the wrong way because of his tendency to be long-winded and circular in his speech. He often made the same point over and over again, which made people check out.

Tom was also a connector—direct, succinct, and equally smart at systems thinking and complicated strategic planning and processes. Tom took delight in refining and driving various structures and policies within the bank, helping teams improve flow and efficiencies that trickled down to the consumer. Like George, Tom's contributions also transformed complexity into simplicity, which parlayed into the financial success of the overall business. The board, in particular, admired Tom's ability to implement fiscal responsibility with innovative and strategic initiatives to improve the bank's bottom line. Tom didn't have a nickname, though. While liked by many, he was known as being a bit cold, sometimes aloof, "all business, no play." Those who were big fans of Tom worshipped his genius, often placing him on a pedestal.

Each time George knew he was meeting with Tom, his stomach churned in anticipation of yet another challenging discussion that involved silences, awkwardness, and flat-out rejection. Although George had previously worked in cultures of constructive confrontation—where people openly communicated about what they didn't like and offered constructive criticism and solutions—his interactions with Tom were like nothing he'd ever experienced. It was as if they couldn't talk with one another. George had tried a number of things to bridge the gap with Tom. He asked questions about Tom's family, trying to learn what mattered to the CFO. Nope. George expressed curiosity—inquiring about vacations, summer plans. Nope. George started conversations about hobbies, interests, food preferences, ancestry, current events . . . and nope. George felt that there wasn't any gap to bridge, just a tall, never-ending wall to scale in the hopes of connecting with Tom better so that he could see this "brilliance" that many people spoke about at the bank's headquarters. They were at a stalemate.

Tom, for his part, was annoyed by George's nosey questions and wished they could skip the small talk. He felt George always needed to start every interaction with chit chat, which he felt was an utter waste of time, especially when his to-do list was giant. Furthermore, Tom's to-do list included important, timely, and complex projects that needed his full attention to see through to fruition. Tom spent most of his energy deep in the bank's data, analyzing earnings and loss reports, transactions, and more, as a way to fine-tune the bank's systems. Whenever George arrived, Tom felt pulled out of his work. He was like a kid trying to count a huge jar of jellybeans and George's inquisitiveness was a distraction, making him forget where he was and forcing him to start over. Tom also felt that, in his role, the stakes were higher because if he didn't analyze the data or systems perfectly, then that would put the entire bank's operations at risk. He had to remain sharp and focused on the numbers, the details, and the nuances of all the bank's structures.

On the flipside, George also believed that the stakes were high in his role because if the IT systems and mechanisms didn't work to support the financial transactions that Tom sought to improve, then the bank would fail, too.

One day, while in a meeting with the CEO, George and Tom disagreed about how to approach solving a problem about the user experience of their updated online loan application system. It was sane enough at first, both chiming in and volleying the discussion back and forth with their unique perspectives and ideas. George told stories to make his point. Tom used data and process-driven charts. When their ideas converged into a choice for the CEO to make, the conversation turned heated, and that's when AMY and their soured Inner Narrators appeared and rode shotgun on both men's shoulders. Tom exploded first: "George—I don't trust that what you're proposing will work when you clearly ignore the numbers and cover the real issues by telling stupid stories all day long. Data doesn't lie. Human error is par for the course. Trust the data."

"You're a real jerk, you know that?" George reacted.

Ouch.

Have you ever experienced this situation? A near-to-total disconnection with a colleague, boss, or someone in your life? Where you struggle so much to bridge the gap between understanding, liking, and respecting them that it leads you down a path where your Inner Narrator has gone sour and tells you many stories to discredit them? The danger is that once you collect enough evidence from what these stories provide—confirming all the things about them that annoy you—you may feel empowered and righteous enough to declare your total disdain and disrespect for them in some form or another.

Happens all the time.

Sometimes we explode like Tom. Sometimes we issue the silent treatment and respond only when absolutely necessary and with minimal effort. Sometimes we drag our feet when working on any project with them. We default to other passive-aggressive tactics[1] like sulking, eye-rolling, sarcasm, and procrastination to convey how much we don't trust or respect them. When we engage in any these behaviors, we're actively damaging the core of any relationship.

So, what's at the very core of any two-party relationship? On the individual level, we know that at least one person embodies psychological flexibility. However, one person does not make a relationship, right?

A relationship is like a bird's nest that both of you are tending. In the center of the nest is a fragile, growing egg that needs to be cared for or it could easily break. In a perfect world, each time you and the other show up to the nest, you inspect the egg for cracks, thin spots, discoloration. You both look to ensure the egg is also safe. Are there any sharp sticks that are poking out and threatening the shell? Is your egg secure enough so that it isn't going to tumble out and smash on the ground?

This is the egg of trust and respect, which should be centered and tended to in your relationship nest. This egg is what keeps you two engaged in the relationship, because if the egg breaks completely, then there is no need for either of you to return to the nest.

In this case, George and Tom are two strong-willed leaders, two different birds from two different flocks. They are struggling in how they connect and build trust when it comes to tending their shared egg of trust and respect. Their nest is strong enough—the bank and their professionalism have built a bed of sturdy twigs for their egg to grow. Essentially, George and Tom are paid to be in the nest together. Their egg is big, too—both men are grownups and can fully acknowledge the other's talents and leadership position within the company. However, both have failed to attend to the strength of the eggshell, which currently holds the qualities of trust and respect. Tom poked their shared egg with a sharp stick when he burst about George's communication style. There is a crack in the egg now, which means that both trust and respect will be impacted.

Like the yolk and the egg white, trust and respect are iterative and interdependent. They can be separated, but they're meant to be together. Think about how trust and respect are interrelated by pondering these two questions:

1. How can I *trust* you if I can't *respect* you?
2. How can I *believe your opinion* if I don't *value what you have* to offer?

This is a familiar situation that we see come up quite often across a variety of industries, offices, and positions.

THE NECESSITY OF TRUST AND RESPECT

Without a doubt, trust and respect are paramount to any discussion about relationship building, people-centric work cultures, employee productivity and engagement, and leadership. Neuroscience and trust researcher Paul J. Zak claims that a culture of trust is the significant game-changer in any organization's ability to keep its pool of talented and skilled people thriving and producing. His research demonstrates that "employees in high-trust organizations are more productive, have more energy at work, collaborate better with their colleagues, and stay with their employers longer than people working at low-trust companies."[2]

Furthermore, it is proven that trust and respect can be lost faster than they are gained.[3] This means that the egg of trust and respect must be nurtured and reinforced throughout the duration of any relationship because, by their very nature, trust and respect are easy to crack and break.

For example, can you remember times when you—or others—unintentionally behaved in ways that turned people off and diminished the level of trust and respect between you? Do any of these scenarios ring true?

1. A colleague from another firm is consistently late to your lunch dates. No matter what time you schedule them, they keep you waiting fifteen minutes because of viable excuses like parking, traffic, meetings running over time, client needs, and other fires to put out. Will you be inclined to keep asking this person to lunch?

2. Your boss promises the moon and rarely delivers. You love your boss—they have lofty ambitions and sometimes you and the team do hit it big, but never as big as the moon they keep talking about. In addition, the salary schedule never seems to improve. Your boss has asked you to work overtime without pay for several months now on an account that is about to "pay off." Do you trust the payoff is coming?

3. Your mother-in-law is sick and has moved into your renovated garage. You've let the office know that stuff at home right now is tough. You may not be on your "A-game." Months go by where everyone has offered you grace—and you are grateful for your team even though you might not express your thanks as often as you could. At a team meeting, you step up to take on critical tasks that need to be accomplished by a particular date. Your cubicle buddy afterward says, "Would have been nice if you could have told us you were able to do actual work now—I've been picking up your slack for weeks and feeling like you don't even notice or care." You had no idea your cubicle buddy felt that way. You're crushed.

This happens to all of us. Some of us may be able to show up and address what has been cracked, but in our experience, too many people stop tending the shared egg in the nest and just keep going about their lives, never addressing the issues, to the detriment of the overall relationship.

Since you can't run around flapping and yelling, "TRUST ME! RESPECT WHAT I DO AND SAY!" you'll need other ways to tend to the shared egg. In addition, trust and respect are experiences, not one-off events. People who earn the trust and respect of others at work often engage in these key behaviors:

1. They "see you" and find ways to show it. Essentially, they meet your fundamental emotional needs to be understood, accepted, and valued as you are.
2. They show up consistently in their professionalism. You can expect them to be nearly the same every time you see them. No crazy surprises.
3. They follow through on what they say they're going to do.
4. They are honest—no hyperbole, little white lies, or faking it.

In the case of George and Tom, they are meeting at least three out of the four traits above. So, what's missing?

We're all aware of the adage "it takes two to tango," meaning that both parties participate in the dance . . . or there is no dance. Is the same true for relationships? Do both people have to nurture the shared egg of trust and respect? Hasn't George tried? Wasn't Tom the one who cracked the egg? Whose fault is it? Who isn't doing his part to keep the shared egg thriving and safe? These questions, or ruminations within our own fractured relationships, slide us into the Drama Triangle, where the shared egg tends to rot.

People often assume that relationships need to be rooted in 50/50 reciprocation, but when you expect equal give and take, that is a trap that psychologists call the "50/50 Myth."[4] Common sense and lived experiences show that most relationships exist on a spectrum of give and take in various degrees.

➤ The Big Aha! ◄

Here's the good news. The shared egg of trust and respect can be tended to and strengthened when at least one person can be fully counted on for showing up clean and curious, with positive intent and care, and enough psychological flexibility to meet the other person where they are at. Then reciprocation usually follows—and you will have a partner tend the egg with you.

How can you foster more trust and respect, easily and efficiently, in your work relationships?

EARLY ROOTS OF TRUST AND RESPECT

Many of us were taught from childhood to employ something called the Golden Rule—*Do unto others as you would have them do unto you*—as a way to be polite, and therefore, show respect, and therefore gain trust and enter a relationship.

It sounds like a great approach to connecting and building trust and respect with people, but the Golden Rule is not a reliable model because not everyone "works" like you might prefer. Not everyone wants to be engaged with and spoken to *your* way. We have different communication preferences that show up in our personalities and presence.

Meet Stephen and Greg, former coworkers who happen to run into each other at the golf course on a humid summer afternoon.

Stephen walked the length of the driving range to greet Greg. "Hey Greg!" he said. "How is your leg?"

Greg had recently torn his Achilles's tendon and it happened to be the first time back on the driving range. Still in his large black plastic boot, Greg said, "Oh, it's my first time out in eight weeks. I've been cooped up at home and just got released to leave the crutches behind. Man . . . it feels good to get out of the house. I have been itching to hit some balls!"

Stephen tilted his head a bit and interrupted: "Yeah, OK, but how is your leg?"

Greg continued to talk about how his vacation had been interrupted and the whole summer had been impacted.

Stephen interrupted again: "Yeah, OK, but how is your leg?"

Then it hit Greg. He had worked for years with Stephen and knew he was a direct communicator, focused on factual, direct responses. He wasn't a small talker, storyteller, or really even interested in personal matters. And when it came to describing feelings, emotions, or anything internal, Stephen never cracked. *Crap*, thought Greg. *That was awkward. Why did I keep blabbering on when I know that answer doesn't work with Stephen?!?! He just wants to hear about my leg.*

Greg gave the answer HE would have liked to have heard, had he been the person asking the question. Stephen was attempting to connect with Greg, but really just wanted an answer about his leg, not all the details about Greg's world surrounding the recovery of his leg. A quick, simple answer, like: *It's tough but getting better—I'm on week 8 of the recovery.*

Now, there is nothing here that either person did "wrong." This example illustrates what Greg could do differently to connect and communicate better to the person we're with most effectively.

Dr. Tony Alessandra and Dr. Michael J. O'Connor proposed an alternative to the Golden Rule, called the Platinum Rule, which is: *Treat others the way they want to be treated.* This rule impacts how you approach the other, placing your focus on the needs and communication preferences of the other person.[5] Based on their research, they wrote: "The focus of relationships (should) shift from 'this is what I want, so I'll give everyone that thing' to 'let me first understand what they want and then I'll give it to them.' "[6]

The Platinum Rule offers a more expansive approach to trust and respect building. Choosing the Platinum Rule over the Golden Rule is an awareness-based personal choice, where you place your needs and preferences aside (but not away . . . think of it like parking them in the garage for a bit) to communicate better, which will ultimately help strengthen the egg in the nest. Greg and Stephen both knew about the Platinum Rule because of their experience in sales, where they meet the customer needs first before their own.

We're often asked if there's a shortcut to building trust and respect. Again, this is fragile and tricky terrain that involves two people, so there's no easy answer. However, we believe that you can use the Platinum Rule as an easy tool to grow trust and respect faster, especially with people you don't know that well, or you think you know but truly don't. To shift your approach from the Golden Rule to the Platinum Rule, you will need to understand how trust and respect are molded by two core qualities that nearly everyone pays attention to in the first critical seconds of any interaction. These two core qualities show up in your communication style, and like most people, you probably have one quality that dominates the other. Do you tend to begin conversations by show-ing *sincerity* or by showing *competency*?

UNDERSTANDING SINCERITY AND COMPETENCY

In all situations, remember that AMY and the Inner Narrator are working in tandem to decide whether you are safe whenever you are with other people—especially if you infer that they are different from you. Plus, whomever you're with, interpersonal neurobiologists agree that within the first seconds of interaction, humans assess the notion of safety: "Can I trust this person and respect them, too?"

Back to Tom and George.

The CEO and the board knew they could not afford to lose these two exemplary executives and called us in to help. After interviewing both gentlemen, both of us took a huge breath. This was a simple gap that was drastically affecting their teamwork. There were no canyons to be crossed. This didn't have to be hard.

We met with both George and Tom independently and they both expressed admiration and respect for each other's skills, ded-ication, knowledge, and the teams they led. There was just one stumbling block: they just couldn't stand to listen to each other. Their styles were mucking it up. The other person had become like an annoying alien to them.

The good news was that in our initial interviews it was evi-dent they both wanted to bridge the gap, collaborate, and be aligned. Both had psychological flexibility, but it had become so lost in their annoyance with one another's communication styles that they had forgotten to tend to their shared egg of trust and respect. We were able to show them how their individual AMY was hijacking them and that their Inner Narrator was building a case of evidence against the other person, delegitimizing the other person's value. We introduced the Platinum Rule and asked if they had put any effort into using that as a navigating tool.

We were met (as we often are) with: "That never occurred to me." Which translated to us as: "I never thought to change my communication style to meet the other person's style."

Then we asked them if they had ever acknowledged that in their attempt to achieve like-minded goals, each led with a different energetic and communication approach.

We were met (as we often are) with: "I knew they were different than I am, but I'm not sure why or how." Which translated to us as: "I know they behave, speak, and act differently than me but I never stopped to think how I might use that to bridge the gap with them."

They had little clue about what we were referring to. Then we said:

"George leads with sincerity to connect and build trust."

"Tom leads with competency to connect and build trust."

"You need both sincerity and competency to make any of your initiatives, designs, and systems work at the bank."

Light bulbs went off.

Then we showed them something simple, based on research and science, that could change the entire way the two of them collaborated to accomplish meaningful work. (See Exhibit 8.1.)

Sincerity	Competency
Likeable	Reliable
Authentic	Knowledgeable
Affable	Accountable
Amiable	Capable

EXHIBIT 8.1 How Sincerity Differs from Competency

Harvard organizational researcher Dr. Amy Cuddy studied the impression that we make on others when we face social pressure. Her research is about how humans infer warmth (sincerity) or how competent someone is within the first critical seconds of any interaction. The field of social psychology points to sincerity and competency accounting for "more than 90% of the variance in our positive or negative impressions we form of the people around us." These impressions come from how we show up, or our *presence*. Presence is the quality of being present without distractions and available to the current moment and/or person that you're with. And presence is also the experience of what people infer and feel about you, often affirmed by the energy that you emote and the knowledge that you display.

Cuddy's research shows that most Americans prefer to build trust with a warm and authentic person who places emotional needs above skills and knowledge. Yet some people prefer to build trust with a person who leads with competency first, essentially showing us what they know and can do reliably. Often these preferences are contextualized by where we physically are (at work or home), who we're with (family or colleagues), and by what we need (a plumber to unclog the drain, a professor to explain the economy, or a comforting mother to ease a broken heart).

So, based on what we need, we unconsciously assess the person's presence by wondering if they have any or all of the qualities shown in Exhibit 8.1.

Plus, like most things, having or not having sincerity/competency is not simply black/white. The qualities of sincerity and competency exist on a spectrum—it's not an either/or mentality—but rather is like walking on two legs. For example, both George and Tom have the qualities of sincerity and competency, even if they don't lead with both at work in how they communicate to build trust and respect.

When you walk, you tend to favor one leg. But if you were to stumble, your other leg would be your natural default to "catch" you. Your second leg may lag or quickly catch up to stabilize you. You need both legs—sincerity and competency—to bring depth and richness to your relationships.

THE EXPERIENCE OF SINCERITY

Sincerity is a presence and often related to the adage "People don't care how much you know until they know how much you care." In this paradigm, trust and respect are built by experiencing honesty with another person, where they appear to be genuine, warm, and will have your back in all situations. Sincerity correlates with the hallmarks shown in Exhibit 8.2.

EXHIBIT 8.2 Six Elements of Sincerity

THE EXPERIENCE OF COMPETENCY

Competency is also a presence and focuses on the knowledge, skills, and credentials of a person. In this paradigm, trust is built by experiencing capability, where they appear to be able to accomplish tasks, are dependable, and have a level of expertise that they can bring to the relationship. Competency correlates with the hallmarks shown in Exhibit 8.3.

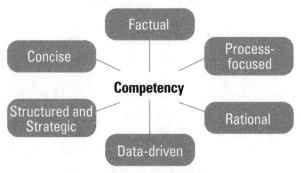

EXHIBIT 8.3 Six Elements of Competency

Can you see Tom?
George?

What about you? Which leg do you lead with first? Who do you unconsciously gravitate toward in relationships? People like Tom or people like George? Does it matter if you're with this person at work, at home, or in the community?

➤ Another Big Aha! ◄

Now that you've identified your preference to build trust and respect, here is the BIG AHA: the burden of quality communication is on you—not the other person. To bridge the gap most effectively, employ the Platinum Rule and lead with the energetic experience of sincerity or competency that matters most to the person you're working with. Put aside your own preference as a strategy to tend to the shared egg of trust and respect.

Bringing light to how we approach people to build trust and respect helps you know how to show up, bridge the gap, have better conversations, and increase your collaboration with someone who carries a different preference than you. It especially works with strangers and people you do not know that well—because you can infer how to lead the conversation in those first critical moments of interaction. When preparing to meet with someone, ask yourself if they lead with a sincerity or competency approach? Shift yours to match and show up as yourself, but with that energy.

For example, let's say you're a fundraiser and you have to meet a philanthropist who has given your cause $50,000 to help ease hunger. They make you nervous. You can tell that this funder cares about data because of how they wrote their funding guidelines, asking you to track several metrics. They will likely want to hear how you moved the needle on hunger using numbers rather than telling a heart-warming story about how your mission helped someone fill their fridge and feed their children. Your preference is to always start with a mission-based story that should break open the hearts of people. Well, your philanthropist has heard all the stories before and is quite numb to the pain your organization has been able to solve. It doesn't mean that they don't want to hear the success story about how their money transformed a person's life, but they want the data first. So, appease their brain and start there; then they will likely be satisfied and relaxed enough to truly hear your amazing story of impact. Lead with the leg of competency and then follow up with sincerity. This helps you strengthen the trust and respect between you—because you gave them what they wanted first.

WHEN IN DOUBT—A WINNING APPROACH

George and Tom turned a corner—and it was quite easy and efficient. We all agreed that there was no need for some convoluted magic elixir. Both men committed to having awareness about their approaches and finding tangible ways to connect with each other (and others). They depersonalized having their preference be the "winner." They acknowledged that everyone has the qualities of sincerity and competency; they just show up in different ways.

Here's what George and Tom tangibly agreed upon.

They would walk into each and every conversation asking for what they need.

George now sets up each meeting with more clarity and a better sense of time: "Tom, let's make an agenda and understand what we want to get accomplished so we can both walk out of the meeting aligned and clear." (Offering respect to Tom and his preferences.)

Tom now steps into each interaction with a warm smile and more patience, willing to hear the stories behind the technical: "George, tell me a little more about what you are hearing and seeing and how you feel this might play out?" (Offering respect to George and his preferences.) In addition, Tom takes the time to inquire about George's life outside of work, and now shares tidbits from his own personal life.

Their interactions are now clearly defined and honor each other's approaches and communication styles and fundamental emotional needs. George needs to be seen as a whole human. Tom needs to be seen for his intelligence and eye toward data.

Remember the first story in this book about Dr. Malcolm and Anne? They had nearly the same issue—both communicated differently while also needing to be seen . . . and spoken to . . . for who they are. Dr. Malcolm needed to be seen as the expert he is—speaking through his vocabulary of chemistry, biology, science, and a patient's needs. Anne needed to be seen as the expert she is—speaking through her vocabulary of creativity, marketing, design, and consumer needs.

And yes, all our clients have reported slippage! We are in our human suits, and it's natural to default to our core behaviors, reactions, and preferences. We remind them, as they remind themselves, that they can choose the Platinum Rule over the Golden Rule, not belittle the other person's preferences and styles, and show up differently to get back on the collaborative road again. Even George jokes with Tom sometimes and says, "Give me a little something, please . . . like tell me where you're going on vacation this year at the very least." Tom can joke with George now and say things like, "Great story, Mark Twain, but please show me the data!"

That's the thing about tending to the egg of trust and respect. The egg hatches and becomes a bird—taking on a life of its own. This indicates that you have a very healthy and strong relationship, where people can be candid with one another without any fear that they're walking on eggshells or smashing valuable eggs.

Finally, a lot of new clients tell us they are nervous about inferring how to show up. We tell them that when in doubt, enact something we've coined *warm conciseness*: It's a friendly attitude with a relaxed presence and clarity of mind. It is clean and caring. You emote warm conciseness when you put aside distractions, from addictive technology to the pressure that steals your attention. Avoid rambles, digressions, and out-loud processing. Listen and ask curiosity-driven questions. Share a little something about yourself, but be focused on the needs of the conversation at hand. Show care in service to your relationships.

Warm conciseness disrupts AMY's chemical cocktail spew and engages your prefrontal cortex with greater creativity and clarity. Warm conciseness bypasses the addiction to stories that aggrandize drama, fuel hyperbole, and promote polarizing either/

or thinking. This grace-like state allows both the brain and the mind (yours and theirs) to safely open up and engage at a deeper level.

Overall, the most successful people we work with constantly adapt and bring the appropriate presence to maximize trust and respect. They understand how to influence people and forge connections. They become the channel. Whether it's building teams, navigating strategies, training new people, creatively exploring new opportunities, or simply understanding small talk around the office, connection begins with your presence—how you show up!

REFLECTION QUESTIONS

* Think about a relationship you have that is fragmented. Is there any way you can apply the Platinum Rule to it to enhance trust and respect?
* Think about someone you interact with daily. Where does their brain's preference lean, sincerity or competency, and how can you shift how you show up for more connection?
* In an upcoming meeting, class, sales appointment, or engagement, who will be in front of you and how can you structure your meeting to that person's sincerity or competency preference?

ACTION ITEM
The Choice: Platinum Rule over Golden Rule

Spend one day observing the people with whom you work the most: spouse, work partner, friend, child, student. Employ the Platinum Rule. How do they lead: with sincerity or competency? When you and they are with other people, how do they show up?

JOIN THE CONVERSATION AND INTERACT ONLINE
#howyoushowupmatters

CURIOUS CONVERSATIONS
Part 1

You are ready to be released from the finger trap despite how uncomfortable that might be. You're ready to talk. You're also well prepared because:

- You understand how critical it is to meet the emotional needs of another—everyone needs to be understood, accepted, and valued or you have little chance at bridging the gap.
- You practice awareness about how pressure impacts your behavior in your human suit. You take personal responsibility to disrupt your reactions when AMY or a soured Inner Narrator hijacks you.
- You view a person and/or situation in a new light by twisting your kaleidoscope, watching how the jewels inside tumble and fall differently to make new patterns, new solutions.
- You refuse to play any of the default behavior roles when you're slid into the Drama Triangle. You step into the Circle of Choice to exit the sharp edges of the triangle with its shame, blame, and toxicity.
- You show up clean and curious to connect, communicate, and collaborate. You shift your conversations into one-way interactions rather than speedy Daytona two-way competitive conversations.

- You jump over your listening hurdles to be present. You choose a clean, curious listening filter rather than the sloppy listening filters.
- You tend to the shared egg of trust and respect by leading with the other person's preference and how they want to be treated, you lead with sincerity or competency.
- You step into the Explorer role to head into the unknown and witness something new: a perspective, idea, belief, value.

Great! You are aware, you are primed, you are optimally prepared for a Curious Conversation.

UBUNTU: WORDS BUILD PEOPLE AND WORLDS

Humans are social creatures and learn to converse by emulating others' language and patterns, typically from one's culture and family of origin. Neuroscientists know that your brain is molded by continuous interaction with people, echoing the African idea of "Ubuntu," which means that a person becomes a person only through other people.[1] And primarily, you acquired a vocabulary and developed communication skills from who you interacted with in your formative years . . . and you continue to develop them through who you interact with today. Your Ubuntu shows up in your nonverbal communication and word choices.

For example, millennials are now the largest generation in the American workforce, replacing the dominant workforce of baby boomers.[2] This generation has grown up on social media, and 68 percent of them prefer texting as their primary form of communication. Many studies say that's because they believe texting is more efficient and avoids wasteful small talk, which they view as a distraction to completing their work. For older generations, texting is often a minefield for miscommunication and unprofessional. You can see Ubuntu in action when you consider that Generation X/Y often prefers email, baby boomers often prefer the telephone, and the "Greatest Generation" often prefers face-to-face interactions. However, as millennials grow into the majority, older generations are expanding their communication skills and reciprocating with text-based messaging to work better together.

Here's another example of Ubuntu in this context: Did you know that younger millennials and Generation Z overwhelmingly believe that responding with the word "OK" is considered rude!?!?! This generation prefers to use "kk" instead to show agreement! Unlike older generations, they believe that "OK" conveys sarcasm and eye-rolling.[3] This is the power of Ubuntu and words. (Pro-communication tip, if you're trying to bridge the gap with a different generation than you're from, use the Platinum Rule and engage with their preferred method of communication! It helps tend to your egg of trust and respect.)

Words are complex and accompanied by hundreds of years of meaning behind them. They are symbolic, shifty, and never neutral. There is often a gap between what someone says and what an ear hears. People interpret words differently depending on the pressure they are experiencing in their human suit. In a conversation, it's often up to the listener to translate the words of someone else into what they can understand. Yet, how often does the listener misinterpret, mishear, or misjudge the intent of the speaker? How often does the speaker feel that language failed them and that the listener missed their intended meaning?

You know the power of words—they can build you up or shred you to pieces. They shape perspectives, relationships, and how someone shows up in the world. Eeyore and Tigger from the beloved *Winnie-the-Pooh* books exemplify this power. Their language and nonverbal communication contribute to their friendships and conversations in the Hundred Acre Wood with Robin, Pooh, and friends. Eeyore leads with melancholy, using depressed, sad language to convey his perspective about the world. Tigger leads with passion, using exciting, flamboyant language to convey his perspective about the world.

People's energy, like Eeyore's and Tigger's, affects people because every conversation you have includes a biochemical reaction. There is always an exchange of energy. When you're in a conversation, your brain will react to their energy within .07 seconds.[4] Their presence and language impact you in less than a single second, and that's fast enough for AMY to kickstart a bio-chemical process, often pushing you to reaction.

How you show up—your energy, presence, questions, words, and nonverbal communication—affects the person or group of people within .07 seconds. They'll either go on the defense, offense, or anything in between. The Curious Conversation structure in this chapter will equip you to derive better meaning from what the other conveys. It's designed to help you figure out what to ask, how to connect, and what to say in response. In a Curious Conversation, your goal is to help ease their brain, meet critical emotional needs, and avoid the hijack.

There are eight "moves" that you can make in the first half of any Curious Conversation. Some of the moves you won't need to make, depending on the person and situation. Some moves you'll spend more time on than others. Try them out and find your balance.

MOVE 1: AVOID MEASUREMENT-BASED QUESTIONS

Wait, *what?* Forget questions?

Isn't the basis of any conversation about the quality of questions we ask one another?

Isn't curiosity about asking questions?

Our answer is sometimes *yes*, but often it's a resounding *no*. Too many people—or rather, too many AMYs and soured Inner Narrators—perceive questions to be judgmental and nerve-racking "interviews." Let's look at the following question words used most often in our daily conversations:

- Who?
- When?
- Where?
- How and/or How much?
- Why?

These question starters are highly valuable and elicit important information, processes, and figures. They clarify confusion, hard numbers, and timelines, and they support strategic decision-making. These question words reveal data. These are important questions and there is a time and place for these questions. Yet there is an unconscious danger in leading conversations with this language in a relationship where emotional needs are on the line. These are measurement-based questions. And measurement often triggers a compare-and-contrast dynamic, which easily places you and the other in a place of competition or debate. Measurement is a form of judgment. In other words, these questions can put the receiver into defense or offense. Ask too many of these questions and it can also become an interrogation where a person has to "get-it-right-or-else" mode.

Showing up curious is not about being a woodpecker full of questions that drill and bore into someone, nor does curiosity push for measurement, comparison, or judgments.

Let's debunk the most popular interrogative of all—the word *why*. You've probably been taught that the most important, most curious, most powerful question in the world is *why*. You have probably been taught that this word elicits deep understanding and truth when used. Well, we hate to break it to you, but in most circumstances, *why* is poisonous. AMY and the soured Inner Narrator become aggressive and irritable with this word. The favorite word of all three-year-olds pushes nearly all of us, from cradle to grave, into a place of polarity, fight or flight, life or death, and love or hate. Pressure often arrives when *why* arrives. Let's demonstrate with a super quick and easy example:

"Hey Robin, why did you miss the deadline?"

"I only got it in a day late," Robin answers with a slightly peeved tone. "I had too many competing projects and had to make a tough choice about which one to prioritize, but at least I got it done."

"Well, a heads-up would have been nice: I could have rearranged some things on the timeline. The client was displeased, and I had to take the brunt. How many times has this happened before?"

"This was only the second time," Robin says, crossing her arms.

"The second time? No wonder they were annoyed. Why didn't you tell me about the last time? When did this happen?"

"Oh, like a month ago, but it was fine. Babs said they're usually chill with a one-to-two-day window. Why are you so upset?" Robin gives a little shrug of her shoulders.

"It wasn't pleasant to talk to them yesterday, and we really need this account. Just let me know next time, so I know how to approach them."

"I will. Sorry about that. I didn't think it was a big deal. They're always pretty pleased with our work." Robin makes a little noise at the end of this sentence, akin to "psssh-whatever."

(Negative energy lingers.)

"Onward we go, I guess. How's the rest of your day going?"

"Fine," she says and looks away from you.

Perhaps you've had a similar conversation. Even though this conversation recovered quickly, leftover negative "residue" infected both you and Robin. You will remember and hold onto the negative residue instead of other positive interactions with her. In worst-case scenarios, relationships that have consistent *why* energy (echoing the suspicious, defensive listening filter) are damaging in the long term, festering into an avoidance of talking to people, the destruction of trust and respect, and burning bridges.

Simply put, people rarely like to explain themselves when confronted with *why*. *Why* throws someone into annoyance and frustration and slides you both into the Drama Triangle, where the questioner becomes the persecutor and the person who answers becomes the victim. *Why* challenges a core question about our emotional needs that we all wrestle with, often unconsciously: "Aren't I good enough?" In Move 3, we will teach you how to replace *Why* with *Tell me about, Share with me,* and *What about* as replacements.

MOVE 2: FINE-TUNING YOUR NONVERBAL PRESENCE

Nonverbal communication is just as important as, if not more than, our actual words. UCLA Emeritus Psychology Professor Dr. Albert Mehrabia's highly quoted study discovered that 7 percent of people allocate a meaningful connection based on language, 38 percent to tone of voice, and 55 percent to other nonverbal behaviors.[5] What's most important in his research is that everything you relay in an interaction must be congruent, meaning that your language, tone of voice, eye contact, presence, and emotions must be aligned throughout the conversation to optimize impact and to bridge gaps most effectively.

This played out between Michael and Trent at the men's fashion company that we introduced in Chapter 4. Neither man could converse and connect effectively and meaningfully because Michael was incongruent with his words and energy. Since he refused to show up clean and curious, it didn't matter what he said because he conveyed bitterness, envy, and disrespect through his tone and energy. Within less than .07 seconds, Trent's AMY knew that he wasn't safe in this interaction. Michael committed curiosity fraud at its finest, so Trent rejected nearly everything Michael said—including the one pathetic "sorry" he mustered near the end of his tenure as a last-ditch effort to keep his job.

When Michael was pissed that Trent didn't accept his apology, he slid right into the Drama Triangle and blamed us. He came at us with, "I did what you said, I used the language you gave me, and I even looked him straight in the eye as I was saying sorry."

Michael was traditionally raised to believe that making direct eye contact is the best way to convey that you're telling the truth. It's likely you've been taught that, too, along with this equation: making eye contact = you're listening and present.

Eye contact does demonstrate engagement . . . however, prolonged, focused eye contact creeps AMY out. Also, too much eye contact creates "performance" pressure, often pushing the speaker to provide a response that is *acceptable*, rather than their truth. This is often a new idea to our clients. So please be mindful of it.

We have found that it's best to not sit across from another person, but off to the corner or to the side. We prefer walks for curious conversations, switching up the office dynamic to energize a dreary routine—and hopefully to reinvigorate the relationship. Being side by side with someone and hearing them, rather than "reading their face," seems to lessen their fear and increases the feeling of safety. If you can't leave the office, see if you can find a quiet space instead of being across a desk. Understand how the balance of power plays out in different spaces. Find a space that is less confrontational. Explore a balance between looking in the eyes, looking away and offering space, and glancing at them occasionally.

For the rest of the moves in a Curious Conversation, we'll illustrate them through two stories so that you can see how it plays out on the team level and in one-to-one interactions. Each Curious Conversation was drastically different, and we hope to showcase how the moves can be applied in different situations.

MOVE 3: USE INVITATIONAL LANGUAGE: *TELL ME ABOUT* AND THE BONUS QUESTION

Remember that a "one-way" Curious Conversation invites the other side to deepen into their thoughts and thought processes, naturally allowing them to share what they want without inserting yourself. Your *I* is not needed—yet. No need to *should, could, or would on the person* in this moment. In this conversation, you do not need to be "seen," or acknowledged, which means that, in this moment, for just a little bit of time, you can suspend your perspective, opinions, and beliefs from lived experiences and emotional needs.

Some people argue that it's impossible to suspend themselves from anything. Of course, you can never escape your human suit. However, we ask those people if they have ever gone to a movie theater, cracked open a fiction book, or enjoyed a theatrical play. They always say, "Of course." Well, that's an act of suspension. You suspend yourself in service of the experience of the story that is about to unfold. You know that the underdog will overcome and transform in the end no matter how much the villain shows up to derail them. When you suspend yourself, you do service to the relationship and shared goal. You choose to enter the story— to step into those perspectives by suspending your own.

You want to be inside their perspective, in their kaleidoscopic patterns, inside their lived experiences, knowledge, values, and sense of identity. And you do it as an Explorer to hear, see, and learn something new, so that you can shift your own kaleidoscope to have a better interaction and conversation.

Cass and Antony are comanagers of a chain of growing boba tea shops that are quickly becoming popular and frequented by working young adults, college students, and teenagers. The stores are known for their chill, beach vibe and welcoming atmosphere. The employees are trained to be chatty and flirty—to act like the customer is one of their friends by inquiring about their daily plans, hobbies, and bucket-list dreams. Their customer service and branding strategy is built around ensuring that every person who enters the tea shops knows that they belong and are surrounded by friends.

Cass is the senior manager, having worked her way up from "tea sommelier" (like a barista). She embodies the vibe and connects easily with most anyone given her charisma and cheerful attitude. Antony worked his way up the ranks, too, and has been partnered with Cass by corporate to help them better train the team to support the explosive growth. He comes from another store in a different part of the city. He also knows how to embody the brand and connect, while also focusing on efficiency, making sure that tea orders are delivered quickly. He is attuned to the danger of having a brand built on all that customer chattiness—extraneous talk can delay orders, hampering the customer experience because they sometimes have to wait 8 to 11 minutes for a drink. He wants to revamp the training program's playbook accordingly. And he's let corporate know his intentions and they agree with him and have given the green light *to increase efficiencies while not affecting the connective tissue of the culture.* As we encounter Cass and Antony, we find the two leaders at an impasse on how to best implement the customer training program with their fifty-two employees.

Emotions and perspectives are running hot. Cass is upset with Antony and his insistence that employees stop walking through the stores, gabbing with customers, and checking in on them. Antony is upset with Cass that she can't see how that distracts from output and impacts the other employee duties, too, like stocking and cleaning. According to Cass, Antony wants to throw out the entire training program because many of his edits include discarding the values of belonging and friendship found within the training playbook. Cass is a bit hurt by this because many parts of the training playbook were based on her when she was considered a superstar in the earlier days. She feels disrespected, and every time they try to work through their issues, miscommunication abounds. The loss of trust and respect has ultimately shifted her perspective of him. He's gone from "The Amazing Antony" to "That A-Hole Antony" in a matter of weeks.

Cass heard us speak at a women-in-business luncheon and asked us to coach her through this challenge, because deep down she knew that she and Antony could be a dynamo team. Plus, she wanted the frustration and anger to end, to be released from the finger trap that kept her up at night and made a job that she loved just plain miserable. She needed to have the tough conversation with Antony about his behavior, though, and given her disposition, she felt ill equipped, too reactive, and just plain nervous.

We taught her the Curious Conversations moves, where the first "question" would be nonthreatening and neurochemically open Antony's mind and his prefrontal cortex, feeding him "feel-good" hormones while downregulating the stress hormone, cortisol. This magical phrase would help him lower his defenses and possibly neutralize the reactive impact of his AMY or soured Inner Narrator.

The phrase is *Tell me about,* and those three words invite the speaker to begin on a topic where they need to begin, rather than being interrogated by direct, measurement-based questions.

One of the reasons why we like *Tell me about* as the invitational opener is that it's malleable and simple enough to convey different tones. It sounds caring, but is not gooey, sappy, or soft. It can sometimes sound precise and analytical. It can sound empathetic and engaged. Other times, the invitation sounds firm and assessing. It can be adapted to leading with either sincerity or competency. When the phrase becomes stale and repetitive, swap out *Tell me about* with *Share with me* or *What about.*

Using these words will be like working a muscle at first and will develop and grow as you experience different interactions. When you start using this technique, it may feel a bit clunky because many of you may be accustomed to the two-way Daytona raceway conversation or filling in the space with your own information and stories. As you increase your skills, it feels better and better, making it a default conversation opener.

Tell me about works for all kinds of conversation starters. It might start small talk with a colleague, prospect, or new client over coffee. It might be used at a meeting with your staff or in a one-to-one with an employee. It might be how you reenter your household at the end of the day and talk with your family. It might be a way to reply to an encounter that has you confused, spinning, and frustrated.

- "Tell me about your weekend."
- "Tell me about your impression of the real estate market today?"
- "Tell me what has you so angry with your manager right now."
- "Tell me about the restaurants that you love, locally."
- "Tell me about your day at home with the kids."
- "Tell me about your strategic plan."
- "Tell me about our new cyber security policy on client patching."
- "Tell me about what's happening in your sales pipeline right now."
- "Tell me about what the data is showing us right now."
- "Tell me what evidence you see that shows your perspective."
- "Tell me what you want to do with your frustrations right now."
- "Tell me what I have done to contribute to this gap we have between us."

At first, Cass resisted: "But won't that allow him to justify his reasons? I need him to see how letting go of our training program is damaging."

"You will use the invitation strategically to find a way into what he cares about when it comes to your shared goal of training the staff to have both quality engagement with your customers and being responsible to achieve the duties of the job efficiently to keep operations smooth. You'll open with a series of *Tell me about* invitations, listening for energy words that you can follow and be curious about in order to better understand what's at stake for him and, accordingly, why he behaves as such. Then you'll be able to respond with what you need, your boundaries, values, and expectations.

Then, if appropriate, you'll collaborate with him to come up with three viable solutions to begin ameliorating your situation."

Cass decided to give it a try. She led the conversation with a competency mindset, meeting Antony's desire to be more efficient with operations, rather than starting with the employee chatter and culture. We warned her that he might show up irritable or angry and may need to "empty his cup" to release some of the pressure he feels, or some pent-up tension aimed at her. The key would be to hear it without taking anything personally and trust that once he spilled some stuff from his very full cup, he'd relax into the conversation. Finally, we also gave her a "bonus point" question to ask near the end of their conversation, which is: *And if there were one more thing to share with me about this topic, what would it be?* This question allows the speaker the chance to utter one more personal truth for them, and often their response turns out to be valuable and illuminating, which sets the stage for part two of the conversation (covered in the next chapter).

We reviewed what happened with her (full disclosure, we never met Antony as we weren't hired by the company, only by her personally) and here's her report of how her Curious Conversation unfolded:

Cass: "I asked him if we could go on a walk. He was suspicious and asked me if he needed to prepare anything prior. I said, 'Nope, I'm hoping to truly hear your perspective about our team.'"

That was a great response and set up because:

1. Cass gave the context of why they were meeting.
2. She kept her answer succinct enough for him to not read too much into it.
3. She set up the expectation that she was there to listen to *his* perspective.

Cass: "I began the walk with *Tell me about how our team can be more efficient to meet both our needs and the customers' needs.* And he was a bit defensive off the bat, saying something like, 'I already told you and you don't like it.' I responded with a smile and said, 'I'm ready to hear them anew.'"

Great job, Cass! By not biting on his tone or taking things personally, she offered a metaphorical olive branch in a show of cooperation.

Cass: "On our walk, Antony told me how annoyed he gets when the work slows down because it falls on the managers to poke staff to step up and do 'chores' that get ignored, things like cleaning and stocking. In particular, he pointed to stores where employees had taken liberties with their chattiness, which he saw as a way for them to avoid their other duties. He told me a story about a subset of stores in the south area where a few key employees were intentionally slacking off and exploiting the culture—choosing customer chattiness and hanging out with their 'friends' over doing the stores' chores. What was interesting to me was that he kept using the word 'chores,' over how we typically refer to the tasks that need to get done on the opening, midday, afternoon, and evening checklists. We don't ever use the word 'chore' at work. So, I followed it and said, 'Share with me the chores that are most important to be done in a store, in your experience?' "

Another great move by Cass. She noticed his word choice of "chore," and positioned that language—his language—to help her better understand what was important to him. We asked her, what do you think you learned in this part of the interaction?

Cass: "I learned that his gripe was not truly about the training program. He values getting s@%t done and that's when I understood how I was minimizing that effort. I made up a story that he wanted to overhaul the training program, and, to my credit, his irritation was so blatant every time we spoke that his blanket statements suggested he was going to throw out the training program. I see it differently now."

We asked her, "Oh! Did you think he was negating your way of doing things when he kept proposing big changes to the training program?"

She nodded. So we asked her, "After hearing what's important to him—his nonnegotiables about the "chores"—do you think there is room for improvement that wouldn't undermine the current customer service strategy?"

Cass: "Yeah. And I see, now, that some of his insistence is rooted in a fear he has about staff not doing enough. He's scared they are slacking off—and probably because of a couple bad apples who chat longer than they need and probably visit with their friends a little too long."

"I think that would be hard for a newly promoted manager, right? He probably wants to make his mark. So, then where did you go in the conversation?"

Cass: "I asked him: 'Tell me about the pieces of our customer service training that are working for you?' I asked him specifically what he likes best about our work culture. I heard many of the same reasons why I love working there, too. Then he said another interesting thing, kind of emphatically toward the end of that question. He said, 'This is my family and like a family we have to work through hard stuff together and get the chores done.' So, then I followed his energy and asked, 'Share with me, if you would, what makes this hard for you in our family dynamic? And because we didn't come from the same family per se, how might we work together better in this one?' "

Cass is a natural at the Curious Conversation. Not once did she make it about her. Not once did she interject with her knowledge, or reasons why they train a certain way. Nor did she replace corporate language over "chores and family." She remained curious.

Cass: "Basically, he said that in his family, he was always the one left to do the chores because everyone was all play and no work in his large family. He said that what would help him be a better comanager is that we don't fall into the 'mom and dad' trap. So, I asked, 'What's the "mom and dad" trap?' And he said he didn't want one manager to become the fun one who focused on our culture, leaving the other manager to focus on the less desirable aspects of being an employee. He told me he needed—and wanted—a real partner. He thinks we can nail both the culture piece and our efficiencies so that customers wouldn't leave due to slow wait times or dirty stores."

We congratulated Cass on making such astute observations in her Curious Conversation. We asked her, "Did you see a path forward in terms of revamping the training curriculum for staff?"

Cass: "I don't even think that's really the issue now. And, just so you know, I asked the bonus point question before we ended our walk: 'If there were one more thing you could share with me about this, what might it be?' And he said, 'I know that I was really irritated with you before and that I probably came off like a whiner, but I want you to call me out when I make mistakes or when I piss you off. Thanks for the walk today, I know that I needed it.' I was shocked. Then I walked with him for eight silent seconds, which I'll admit was hard for me because I wanted to let him know that I wasn't angry anymore. However, I could sense that he respected the silence. After that I said, 'Thanks for sharing, Antony. I appreciate you. I trust and respect your point of view and am looking forward to being a better comanager with you.' But frankly, I was shocked at how the whole thing went down. I really thought we were going to have to battle it out."

Well, we weren't shocked. This is what happens when you practice *curiosity over criticism* with people. Curiosity in this form invites people to engage rather than inciting more anger, frustration, or division. Think about how Cass could have easily taken this situation and shown up in her irritation and potentially used her seniority against him. She could have asked questions tied to what *she thought* their argument was about, like these:

- "Why are you trying to eliminate the best thing about our stores? People come for the friendship they experience, and if their drink is slow to come, it's fine because at least they're entertained by staff."
- "What is your real issue with our training program? I've been using it for years and that's why the stores are blowing up and so successful and why you were promoted in the first place to work alongside me."
- "I agree that we could improve our efficiencies and clean up better, but how much will that hurt the time our team spends with customers?"

If she had led this conversation with her thought process, which was molded by her diagnosis of the problem—the training program—then she might continue to misunderstand what his real concerns are, where they stem from, and how she could better support him in their shared goal to keep the boba tea shops successful.

In the next chapter, you'll learn how Cass replied with her thoughts and feelings and found a way forward.

Now, let's return to the afternoon portion of the healthcare association's PAC delegation event from Chapter 6 to witness how a Curious Conversation plays out at the team/group level between two warring parties. We will see what happened while also illustrating more moves that you might make within the first half of a Curious Conversation.

MOVE 4: EMPTY THE HUMAN CUP

Imagine a cup filled to the brim. There is no capacity left in the cup—whatsoever—for more liquid.

Imagine yourself as this cup, overflowing with perspectives, preferences, lived experiences, and emotions. Pour in the snarls of pressure, AMY, and a soured Inner Narrator, and it's no wonder most people default to reactive speech, especially when we struggle to communicate inside a cup that is simply too full for anything else to manage.

There is a common phrase used in relationship-building work: *pour into me so I can pour into you.* Which means a margin is required in our human cups. Showing up clean and curious means that you also take responsibility for the fullness of your own cup. The cleaner and emptier your cup, the more connective energy you'll show up with in service of the relationship. However, if your "I" barges in with grudges, negativity, or curiosity fraud, you'll mess up the encounter with your own spillage, tainting the experience. Being in a *we* mindset always means setting aside the self-centered *me.* Biology disruption tactics will absolutely help you empty your cup, at least marginally, so you'll have room when someone else needs to empty theirs.

In a Curious Conversation, you will likely engage with someone's very full cup. They may not have the skills, awareness, or energy to come with a cup ready to be poured into by you. The other person may have to empty their cup by expressing something with one of the core human emotions: anger, fear, sadness, or joy. They may need to vent, process out loud, or give you a piece of their mind to release the pressure. And they need to do this because it will help disarm them and enable them to be more open to answering your invitational questions.

In Cass and Antony's situation, this move didn't really show up because Cass did a good job setting the simple expectation about their walk when Antony asked if he needed to prepare anything with a suspicious voice. However, there may be times when the other person is riled up and that was what happened on the afternoon with the healthcare delegation.

Healthcare Delegation Meeting: Part 2

We broke the delegation members into two teams, red and blue, in two online breakout rooms. Katie (the more liberal-identifying leader) took the red group, and Jennifer (the more conservative-identifying leader) took the blue side.

"Give it to me," we each said in our own rooms, setting a countdown digital timer on the screen. "Tell me what is 'wrong' with the other side. You won't offend me—let loose—you have five minutes. I'm listening."

Surprisingly, neither team took the full five minutes to bark insults, gripes, or frustrations at us. Of course, they hurled some stereotypical labels and insults our way, and that was okay given the rules for emptying their cup. As facilitators, we didn't react— we only allow ourselves to respond with smiles or nonthreatening laughter. We're very clear that our role as facilitators is to be as clean and curious as we preach, dumping any of our baggage prior to being present with them. We also actively choose to care and love the people in the room, even when they are strangers, even when they are resistant and suspicious, even when they engage in poor behavior and negative reactions. Everyone belongs in the room or breakthroughs can't happen.

After their cup was emptied, they were ready for their invitational prompt for the afternoon's townhall.

"Tell me about what it means to be a member of your political party and share a short story from your lived experience that exemplifies both the values of your party and your beliefs. Bonus points if you can tie your story to the events of the past year and why you support certain lawmakers. You'll have fifteen minutes to free write—and I encourage you to write from the heart, be willing to share specific details of your life instead of falling into vague generalities. People connect with vivid details not vague and empty clichés, so if you want to make something stick, write with details that engage the five-senses: sight, smell, touch, feel, or taste, and be specific about your particular lived experience."

We went through a couple of examples, and they were on their way, scribbling down stories.

MOVE 5: LISTEN FOR ENERGY WORDS

After the delegation wrote, we asked them to share their stories aloud with their team before entering the townhall. We asked each delegate to remain in Explorer mode, following the rules of engagement as they listened. They were to jot down any language that struck them as curious or words or phrases that carry a subjective meaning to them.

For instance, in Cass's Curious Conversation, she was struck by Antony's word choice of "chores," and then his accompanying references to "family" when it came to describing for him what was important in their culture. That struck her and resonated with her enough to be curious about his choice of language. When she followed that track of his thinking, you are aware of what unfolded and how that shifted their relationship.

When you're in a Curious Conversation, you'll be listening cleanly and closely to what the other is expressing. Your job is to hear words that convey their values, beliefs, emotions, and personal truth. Don't get caught up in the drama or minutiae of their story. Notice when someone goes dark or numb, or when someone lights up. Listen for the energy behind the words. When they wind down their response to your invitational question, repeat the *Tell me about* phrase (or swap it out with *Share with me* or *What about*) and then use the energy word(s) to keep them speaking so you can gain deeper understanding.

We heard many energy words like *freedom, power, integrity, personal choice*, and *community* with the delegates in our break-out rooms prior to the townhall. Each of those words represented something different for the speaker who uttered them. Their meaning was rooted in their lived experiences, unique perspectives, and values.

Consider that these energy words represent big jewels in someone's kaleidoscope, creating different patterns that impact how they communicate and behave. This matters because people carry their values with them. When values, lived experiences, and unique perspectives overlap and combine into a pattern in their kaleidoscope, they create a "consciousness," also known as a filter for how they view, interpret, and engage with others in the world.

For instance, a person with class consciousness understands most things by looking at them through a lens of class stratification, making decisions based on their own class and assumptions about wealth and power. A person with a racial justice consciousness may be motivated to challenge all forms of hierarchy and history differently than someone who is not attuned to issues of race.

You carry a consciousness with you, too. Are you aware of how your lived experiences, unique perspective, and values color your relationships? If so, how do you feel when someone challenges you about it, or entirely ignores how you see things? Likely you feel irritated, angry, defensive, dismissed, disrespected.

►◄ The Big Aha!

In listening for energy words, try to find people's "big jewels" that influence their kaleidoscope through which they view the world. Deepening your understanding about them helps tend to the shared egg of trust and respect. It actively shows that you're twisting your own kaleidoscope to see them in the new light of their values. Respecting these big jewels helps meet their fundamental emotional needs and builds a solid bridge to meet them across the gap.

MOVE 6: THE POWER OF EIGHT SECONDS

Hold your tongue for eight full seconds. Disrupt the urge by counting one Mississippi . . . two Mississippi . . . three Mississippi . . . .

There are many eight-second rules in life. They apply to golf, bull riding, attention spans, eighties movies, and more. As former public-school educators, we were both taught the power of pausing for eight seconds after we pose a question to students to allow space for everyone to think and then respond. In the workplace, eight seconds is a strategic tactic that you can use in most of your conversations and a great rule to introduce to the conference room. Eight seconds slows anyone's freight train of incoming thoughts, allowing you—and others—to better process what was shared.

In a Curious Conversation, it's a space where you honor what was said by being quiet—conveying to the other that you're letting what they shared sink in—having allowed them to pour into your human cup. This is an empathetic moment, too, because in the silence you are simply *with* them.

These eight seconds can be biologically rough because humans are so hungry to chime in and respond. Don't forget the listening hurdles and disrupt those to better stay in the eight seconds of silence. Most people are not fans of waiting in anticipation, nor being in ambiguous and uncomfortable silence. We feel the urge to fill the silence because it's awkward and most people have been conditioned to speak immediately.

Depending on what was shared, you may want to contribute your own story and feelings to share how you relate, and while there is positive intention behind this desire to connect, suppress it and wait eight seconds. The danger is that you will either:

1. Conflate your lived experiences with theirs, which can misfire.
2. Inflate or deflate what they said with your own interpretation, which can misfire.
3. Negate what they said by erasing their emotions, concerns, fears, and more by offering stories that don't honor or respect their opinions, big kaleidoscope jewels, or what they're going through.

Simply allow what they said to impact you and sink in.

Eight seconds is about *being with* them. That's it. It's your silence and presence that responds with "I hear you." It's a powerful and empathetic action.

Often, people mess up the notion of empathy by lumping their feelings and lived experiences with the other's feelings to show care and connection. That's confusing empathy with sympathy. Empathetic talk often has good intentions behind it—saying things like "I've been scared, too" or "I'm sorry you're feeling that way, I remember being angry, too."

Feelings and emotions are unique to individuals. Denying people their uniqueness and individuality is often what causes the gap to widen in the first place. At all times, we are unconsciously asking if others understand, like, accept, value, and/or respect us—as-is, right now, in our unique identity. Not jumping in with your stories, response, or need to change or shift them during those eight seconds shows respect and helps you avoid falling into the precarious traps of empathetic talk. Eight seconds says without words:

- "I hear what you said and respect it enough to not conflate my feelings and stories with yours."
- "I've allowed what you expressed to take up precious space and I value your thoughts."
- "I trust that what you said is true and have no need to poke holes in it, add to it. What you shared is sufficient."
- "You have made me pause and think in your uniqueness."

When we practice this with our clients, they all report feeling remarkably seen, heard, understood, and valued after someone extends "the grace" of eight seconds. Because, think about it, when was the last time you shared something meaningful and were met with immediate reaction or a response by someone trying to share their perspective, fix the situation, and offer advice? When they conflated, inflated, deflated, or negated what you shared by interpreting it wrong? What would it feel like if what you said was sufficient and accepted, as-is? No other input needed. How might that feel?

We gathered the delegate teams of red and blue together. We reviewed the rules of engagement and asked that four people from each side be prepared to share their stories. After each brave soul shared, we would pause for eight seconds, allowing their unique perspective and lived experience to sink in.

MOVE 7: WHAT RESONATES: RESPECTING DIFFERENCE

We told the delegates that this townhall listening session was not about reaching a compromise. Nor was it about shifting them from one party identity to another. It was about hearing and understanding a spectrum of diverse perspectives and lived experiences—to witness the many variations of what it means to be an American. These dual choices we're faced with in a two-party system is polarizing and destroying the nation. It makes the brain split. It makes AMY more protective and defensive. As adults, we resist change and choose comfort. We build and shape our world to our liking—finding all kinds of evidence and language to defend who we are. Debate and competing choices do little for connection, innovation, creativity, or collaboration.

We heard powerful stories about people's lived experiences and values and how they show up in their politics and communities. They shared stories of their constituents with details that resonated deeply with everyone. After eight seconds of silence, delegates were allowed to respond only to the following two questions, which are derived from our writing practice based on the Amherst Writers and Artists Method.[6] After each speaker shared and there was eight seconds of silence, we asked:

- "What words, images, or details struck you?"
- "What will stay with you?"

They were not allowed to offer back anything that wasn't shared from the person—no ideas, opinions, personal stories. The "feedback" went like this:

> "When you spoke about the crying grandmother in the coffee shop who lost her brother. That will stay with me."

"What resonated for me was when the speaker told us about their version of freedom and what it took for her to fight for it in her town. I get that."

"That moment when the speaker said, 'I want my son to not be afraid to walk the streets at night.' "

The truth is that it's hard to deny someone their humanity, opinion, or belief system once you know them at a deeper level. It's hard to stereotype, label, and negate someone's identity once you know the big jewels that shape the patterns and their consciousness in their kaleidoscope.

In a Curious Conversation, respect their difference. Honor it by acknowledging it and accept them: as-is.

MOVE 8: THANK YOU

In an individual one-to-one Curious Conversation, after eight seconds of silence you will say thank you. Offer a simple *thank you for sharing* before you move into your response.

Remember Cass's response? "Thanks for sharing, Antony. I appreciate you. I trust and respect your point of view and am looking forward to being a better comanager with you."

Terrific.

With the delegates, we asked them to respond to this question as we closed the day: *What do you leave here with?*

Here's a smattering of what we heard:

"I had no idea . . ."

"I feel like I finally understand why the other side says what they do . . ."

"I don't know what just happened, but something has changed inside me—it doesn't change my thinking, but something has softened inside me."

"I never knew . . ."

"I leave here with hope."

Months later, we checked in with leadership of the delegation and they reported these outcomes:

- Increased, positive engagement, which has helped the delegation do a better job of collaborating to move the needle on issues that impact the healthcare industry.
- A safer environment to discuss PAC contributions to certain elected officials and why or why not they would be moved to donate to them.
- They can openly disagree without devolving into polarizing dynamics.
- Healthier communication patterns all around.

Many people rarely experience a Curious Conversation dynamic. A Curious Conversation can focus a situation that's gone off the rails. It can make someone feel heard, seen, and valued when another honors their perspective without interjections. It is a game changer.

Start with a Curious Conversation and be amazed at how it helps you traverse the hard stuff later, when you must give honest feedback. When your response doesn't align with them. We promise you that if you learn to respect difference, then trust will follow, allowing you to openly communicate in the future about nearly anything. And respecting difference costs you nothing—don't fear losing your identity over acknowledging someone else's. Because the truth of the matter is that *wherever there is real trust and respect, there is an underbelly of care supporting it*—and you can't care about someone if you've labeled or stereotyped them, if you don't really *know* them.

In the next chapter, you'll read about the second half of a Curious Conversation where you respond and dialogue.

REFLECTION QUESTIONS

- How full is your cup on Monday mornings? On Thursday afternoons? What is swirling inside (looping and hijacking you) that impedes you from being fully present or engaged?
- What do you notice about your nonverbal cues? What is your eye-contact approach and where can you see a place to shift it to a more neutral place?
- Where do you ask questions that squeeze people instead of open people? Where might you use *Tell me about* as a strategy for engagement?

ACTION ITEM
The Choice: Curiosity Over Criticism

Go have a Curious Conversation and make the moves. Remember to suspend yourself—no need to be seen, heard, or acknowledged in your conversation.

JOIN THE CONVERSATION AND INTERACT ONLINE
#becurious

CURIOUS CONVERSATIONS
Part 2

After thanking the speaker for their thoughts, where will you take the conversation now that it's time for you to respond?

Remember that the purpose of a Curious Conversation is for you to learn something new to better understand, value, and/ or respect the speaker. The purpose is to bridge the gap and to move your collaborative work and relationship forward. How you respond in this moment depends on how much they emptied from their cup, where the conversation landed before your eight seconds of silence, and what, if anything, is being asked of you.

Regardless of what you say, it's worth a reminder that however you respond, your words may be taken as a form of input or advice. As you've learned, AMY and the Inner Narrator are rarely fans of instructions or incoming advice. AMY might spew chemicals and hormones that hijack the other person's executive brain, robbing them partially of the ability to process anything more. The Inner Narrator might be feeling self-conscious, embarrassed, nervous, or sarcastic, obscuring how you'll respond. And remember, nobody likes being pushed, shoved, or cajoled into a solution.

The speaker will land somewhere on the spectrum of being resistant to being ready to hear what you have to offer. Only they, and they alone, can shift to readiness. At the end of the day, you can't really force anyone to behave differently or make changes (even if you are their boss). If you intuit they are in resistance, now might not be the time to offer your thoughts. If you intuit that your relationship is improving and they are approaching readiness, and/or are ready, now might be the time to respond. Sometimes your intuition doesn't matter—because you need to accomplish work and there really isn't time to stay in Explorer mode.

However, you can respond in a way that offers new ways forward and includes them as an active participant.

SHIFTING FROM EXPLORER TO WAYFINDER

Being in this second half of a Curious Conversation can be tricky, which is why we encourage you to shift from being an Explorer to a Wayfinder.

Being a Wayfinder means that you're still being clean and curious but shifting your focus to find ways to move the speaker, relationship, and/or your collaborative work forward. In wayfinding, you're becoming a trusted thought partner and strategic ally. Wayfinding might look like:

- Empowering the speaker to find their next steps, solutions, or answers and processing through them, together
- Helping the speaker identify their options, areas for growth, or ways to focus their energy, strengths, and skills
- Clearing a path forward using transparency, fairness, honesty to support them and your relationship
- Creating conditions for successful communication between you two so that you can accomplish shared goals, together
- Encouraging them to twist the jewels in their kaleidoscope to see different patterns, possibilities, and outcomes

Wayfinding is not about being prescriptive or dogmatic in directing the speaker with reactions, fixes, or advice that radiates with *should, would,* and/or *could* language. Often people intuit *would, should,* and/or *could* as pressure, coercion, disempowerment, or judgment. That language can fracture the strong connection you've fostered thus far in the Curious Conversation.

Wayfinding—at its absolute best—is about responding with language that invites the speaker to further and/or deepen their engagement with you. Your response is both energizing and productive.

Over time, you'll strengthen your wayfinding skills. At first it may feel clunky, or out of your element given your personality.

If you feel that your wayfinding skills are below par, for whatever reason, always rely on giving responses that are in service to fostering more trust and respect in the relationship while remaining true to what you absolutely need to say. If you remain clean and curious, and warm and concise, you will be able to respond better than most folks.

One brilliant way to strengthen your wayfinding skills is to begin your response with "The Ask," which helps guide what you offer back.

THE POWER OF THE ASK: HOW CAN I SHOW UP FOR YOU?

How you engage and respond next will vary depending on what the speaker shared. Maybe they will ask you to reciprocate and share your thoughts, advice, stories, or ideas. Maybe they won't ask directly, yet you intuit that they'd like you to reciprocate and contribute something meaningfully. It might be an appropriate moment to collaborate and come up with options to move them or your work forward, together. Or perhaps your position requires you to give constructive feedback and you feel that they are ready to receive and integrate it, especially if they've emptied some of their human cup.

There is remarkable value in *asking* the speaker how they want you to engage before contributing your thoughts. We acknowledge that this can be odd to people, yet by asking, you are requesting to be invited in as a thought partner about their needs. The core question of The Ask is: *How can I show up for you in support of what you've shared*?

The Ask can easily be adapted to your situation and style. Here are some examples:

- The speaker indicates they'd like some perspective building: *May I share some thoughts with you in support of what you may be experiencing?* If it feels natural, you may add, *Feel free to decline, no pressure!*
- The speaker has shared something meaningful that needs further processing: *How would you like me to show up right now? I'm glad to continue listening or would it be helpful for me to reflect back what I heard?*
- The speaker indicates that they want a "devil's advocate": *What role can I take on to help you think through this better? Would you like me to view it from a particular position or angle?*
- The speaker wants—and or needs—feedback with options: *I think I see a path forward given what you've shared. May I share a couple options that may work, and then we could come up with some, together?*

Overall, when you ask the speaker, *How can I show up for you?*, you're actively prioritizing them in the conversation. You've also provided the other person with the best chance at feeling psychologically safe to communicate and collaborate with you. As a Wayfinder, you will shape your ask depending on the path that unfolds before you. Here are the top five paths that most people face in Part 2 of a Curious Conversation:

1. Twist Kaleidoscopes, Together
2. Coauthor Three Options
3. Define Conditions of Success
4. Give Authentic Feedback
5. The Curious Conversation Is Complete. Nothing To Add.

PATH 1: TWIST KALEIDOSCOPES, TOGETHER

The speaker has indicated they would like your mentorship, stories, advice, thoughts, input, and more. Help them twist their kaleidoscope and make it as little about you as possible. While you might share a small nugget of how you relate to this, the core focus is in using the kaleidoscope for the speaker's growth.

So, you're with Jackie, again, the vegan cupcake lady from Chapter 3. It's been three months since you baked her vegan cupcakes, and to your delight, they were delicious and easy to make. Surprisingly, you adore Jackie now and have become walking buddies on your breaks. How times have changed! You enjoy her unique perspective and aren't threatened anymore. She's still adjusting to the culture in your office and struggling with some strong personalities. One of the issues she frequently speaks about is her disgust with the daily fast food run that Keelan makes for several colleagues who don't bring their lunch to work. At least once a day, either Keelan and his crew or Jackie say something passive-aggressively. Sometimes it's in "good fun," and sometimes it's "veiled judgment." And it comes from both sides. From the smell of the food, to jokes about eating like rabbits and the way Jackie has to defend her protein intake, to her telling them how they're headed into an early grave . . . it's exhausting.

Jackie continuously rails about Keelan and the crew on your walks and it's getting to you because you think fast food is fairly harmless and a personal health choice. And you're witnessing a toxic dynamic take root in the office—many of your colleagues are shunning or avoiding Jackie because they feel judged. You decide to have a Curious Conversation with her to understand her health choices better in the hopes of helping bridge the gap between her and your coworkers.

You begin the first part of the Curious Conversation with *Share with me your reasons for being so health conscious. I'm curious, where does this come from?* From there she unleashes, and you learn by following the energy words that her entire kaleidoscope is colored and patterned by health—from how she was raised on a farm, to becoming a competitive athlete in college, to losing her dad to cancer, to caring about her environmental footprint. Veganism is a big jewel in her kaleidoscope and her passion for it bleeds into nearly everything, including how she shows up at work.

After you thank her for sharing, she says, "I know that I can really annoy people—I mean, I'm not dumb. I know what people think of health nuts like me. Remember when you made my cupcakes and they turned out to be one of your favorites, though? I wish more people were open and accepting like you."

Inside you chuckle because she really has no idea how resistant your Inner Narrator was to her—and her vegan cupcakes. So, you make The Ask: *May I share some thoughts with you in support of what you may be experiencing with others in the office? It's okay if you don't because it might be hard to hear. No pressure, I'm here for you.*

"Of course," Jackie says. "I want to know! I don't mean to turn people off, I just don't understand what the big deal is about making healthier choices."

"In my lived experience," you explain, "I have struggled to connect to people like you, who deeply care about health, in particular. You're one of the first people I've been able to bridge this gap with—so thank you for pushing me to be open. Most of the guys in the office—and I know you know this—don't carry this same health consciousness that you do. Many of us were raised on fast food, and it *is* inexpensive and quick when you need it to be. It's easy—and easy works for the majority of folks. From our interaction about the cupcakes last winter, I know that it isn't your intention at all to shame anyone for their health choices. And health is a very personal issue—at least it is for me.

"But as someone who loves butter, sugar, and honestly, fast food, I struggle to not beat myself up when I'm with someone who is so fit, strong, and monitors their nutrition. I fall into the trap of comparison and contrast . . . and that makes me react unkindly to people like yourself, especially if I don't really know them. I know that you're not pushing an agenda on anyone—and you have every right to be who you are and eat how you wish. What I see happening in the office is concerning me—they are turning away from you because they simply feel shamed when you announce your health consciousness in certain ways. I think shifting your focus from commenting upon, questioning, or bemoaning their food choices might improve your relationship with them overall. In making this shift, I think there are some things we could do, together, to show them that you're just the "friendly office vegan" and mean no harm. If this feels possible then I'm here to help. What are your thoughts?"

As the wayfinder on this path, you're validating a big jewel in their kaleidoscope while also connecting for them how you and others' may view it within their own patterns. You're being honest while helping them twist their kaleidoscope.

Jackie says, "Thank you—I know that I see the world differently. I try to be a sensitive person, but I guess I don't realize the way I alienate people with my passion. I'm open to your ideas—you're such a good baker and they really respect you."

PATH 2: COAUTHOR THREE OPTIONS

The speaker has indicated that they would like your support in coming up with ideas about what they could do to improve their situation and/or your work together. It can be easy to become excited and begin piling your ideas on them with *You should do this . . . you should do that*! Many people call this being *should on*. As we've learned in Chapter 5, rarely does AMY or the Inner Narrator like being *should on*, or given instructions, especially if they don't have positive information, or any information, sitting in their limbic system files about your terrific ideas. It's more empowering for them to author their own set of viable solutions—options they can choose from . . . even when their ultimate decision may impact you.

Everyone likes to feel in control of their options, choices, and ultimate future. Our brain and mind take comfort when we have the freedom to choose what's right for us. One of the most powerful ways you can show up for the speaker is to be a Wayfinder who coauthors options with them. How you present their options is important because research demonstrates that the number of choices that a person is presented with impacts his or her brain's ability to reach a decision. Scientists at Caltech speak to the real power of "choice overload," a phenomenon that happens when people are confronted with too much.[1]

Let's explore the power of options and choices and the "magic" number you'll help them coauthor to ease their brain and let them be in power.

Offering One Option: The Pressure Choice

When people are offered a single solution to a problem they're encountering, they tend to experience that as external pressure, perceiving it as being pushed into a corner. Similar to being *shoulded on*, AMY and the Inner Narrator may fight against this approach. One option might sound like:

- *"After listening to your problem, here is what you should do."*
- *"Because of what you shared, this is about the only solution I can see."*
- *"That is crazy stuff . . . here is what I would do."*

These words can cause unnecessary irritation or judgment. How did the sentences make you feel? Make it personal for a minute—be on the receiving side of when someone who was struggling to understand, like, and/or respect you offered you a sentence like that. It triggers resistance, no matter how valuable the wisdom or when there really seems like there is only one viable solution.

The brain and mind, when presented with only one choice, can feel trapped, caged. Often, the person will automatically reject the idea. Offering your best choice, too quickly, can undo some of the hard work you've put into the curious conversation thus far.

Remember this: *Even if this option is the clearest, most logical, and best option, it will feel like being backed into a corner. Save it for later.*

Offering Two Options: The Polarizing Choice

You might think that instead of *shoulding on* them with one option, offering two options would be a better path. However, when someone is asked to decide between two valid options, the pressure is different but still present and strong, causing stress or anxiety. Two options can feel like an ultimatum, deciding between two things that the person cares about, two things where the person has to judge one to be better. The mind splits. The Inner

Narrator has a hard time deciding between the "wrong" choice and the "right" one, even when both could work. It's like asking a kid which parent she likes better: Mom or Dad? Dark or milk chocolate? Savory or sweet? Each option often has its own merits, strengths. Choosing between two options potentially creates frustration and *analysis paralysis* around the decision, placing the speaker into the "stuck" position.

Sometimes, the other person will volley it back to you and ask for the "right" answer, deferring to your preference. That is not helpful, either! The other person needs to choose their own option to have the best chance at being successful. Two options might sound like:

- To your manager: *"As I see it, you can fire him or keep putting up with the issue."* Feels like an ultimatum.
- To your lunch buddy: *"You want Italian or Sushi?"* Hemming and hawing ensues.
- To your sales team: *"You like this updated logo or the old one that has only the new company colors?"* Frustration follows as everyone struggles to choose between updated or revised.
- To your customer: *"Would you prefer to buy this bear stuffy or that rabbit one for your toddler?"* They imagine the temper tantrum of their toddler deciding between which stuffy and decide to buy neither, avoiding another stuffed animal purchase.

Similar to one option, two options can reek of pressure and create havoc unless the person is already pretty clear and ready to make a choice. Often, they aren't. Two options results in comparison and contrast, and sometimes a FOMO—"fear of missing out"—if they can't have both.

Hold on to this point: *Offering two options might seem to be a good way to clear the path forward for the other person, but too often it polarizes and causes feelings of being in an ultimatum, on a seesaw of comparison and contrast, and/or a situation in which if the person chooses one, they will miss out on the other and experience regret.*

Offering and/or Coauthoring Three Options: A Better Choice Emerges

When someone has three distinct options it has the power to relieve pressure. Instead of being pushed into a choice with only one or two options, now there is "pull" energy as one option usually emerges as the better choice of the bunch. Three options sounds like:

- In a performance review, a leader can use three options to help create clarity:

  - *Do you want to continue down the same path and do nothing about your performance and leave the role?*
  - *Do you want to write up an action plan to get back on track?*
  - *Do you want to find a mentor to gain some insight and motivation about how you can improve and what might be possible?*

- In a sales discussion, a representative can explain three ways to be involved in the business:

  - *Use the product.*
  - *Share it with friends and get a discount.*
  - *Build a business and earn monthly commission.*

- With a stubborn teenager before bed who has failed to do their homework:

  - *Well, don't do your homework and pay the consequences.*
  - *Hop on the video tutorial and follow their instructions step by step.*
  - *Want to do it together? Happy to help.*

It's important to note that in a perfect world you remain in curiosity and ask them to share with you what they see their options to be before you offer yours. Likely, though, they have asked you for your ideas. Here's some wayfinding tips:

- *Before I offer mine, what options do you see yourself having? I'd love to walk through them with you and see how they are similar or different.*
- *Are you open to some options that may change things?*
- *Thank you for sharing. One option you always have is to do nothing. How does that sound?* The "do nothing" option is always an option, and there is great power in posing it as their first choice. It's similar to a rhetorical question— one that can be answered with "duh." However, asking the speaker if they want to do *something* rather than *nothing* helps shift them out of any resistance they have left. It allows the speaker to choose their engagement going forward. So, when you don't have three options to coauthor with them, pulling out this option first is great.
- Another option to present, if appropriate, is always, *You can sleep on it, and if you want, we can talk about it tomorrow or when you're feeling ready or clearer.*

Overall, don't be tempted to entertain too many options because that will feed the feeling of being overwhelmed, dialing up the pressure. In wayfinding, boiling down their choices to three options helps clear the path forward. Talk through options with them. Guide the other person to find his or her own additions and subtractions.

Here's what happened when Sammy and Chao, five-year veterans in the sales department of a mobile device company, struggled to connect over Chao's deliberate absence at weekly team meetings. When the boss checked out, Sammy stepped up to bridge the gap with her missing-in-action colleague and used the options path to reconnect.

Chao was by far the team's commercial "rockstar" and led with boisterous and confident energy. Sammy was also a powerful player and led the team by constantly looking for how she might mentor, support, and build her fellow sales leaders up. Both Chao and Sammy were focused on one goal: exceeding the sales quota to earn quarterly bonuses. They went about achieving this goal differently. The tension in the office was building so Sammy asked Chao out for lunch to have a Curious Conversation to better understand Chao's negative quips, his dripping sarcasm, and his lack of attendance at the weekly sales team meetings.

As they sat for lunch, Sammy asked Chao to share with her what was happening with his pipeline. Before Sammy could say anything more, Chao pretty much lost it. He ranted about two core concerns: the quality of poor and unqualified leads, and his irritation with their fellow coworker Kim. He believed Kim was the "weak link" and reason why the team weren't getting their bonuses: "Kim is dragging the team down and a waste of time and energy."

Chao, hijacked by AMY and an Inner Narrator turned into attack dog, continued to unload for the next ten minutes. Sammy allowed Chao to empty his very full cup without interjection. Sammy reported that she had to practice lots of breathing and disrupting her own Inner Narrator as she focused on clean listening because she wanted to interject and dialogue with him. She wanted to defend Kim, talk about her leadership on the team and what she was trying to accomplish, and ask him directly to let it go and return to the sales meetings. She remained silent and followed Chao's energy words.

She's glad she did because it allowed her to hear two threads dominating Chao's complaints: a lack of leadership and strategic sales pipeline structure. What she hears is that this has created a dynamic in the team that has bred insecurity, kept people in silos, and has broken the team spirit. As Chao wound down his tirade, releasing negative energy from his very full cup, Sammy asked the bonus question: "And if there were one more thing?"

He responded "Look, I know I am putting the blame on Kim, but it isn't just her fault. I can't stand that Paul [the boss] isn't around anymore to give us guidance. I mean, WTF, it's not my job to step up and lead a team, it's his team. Above my pay grade. It's all gone sideways and when I sit in those weekly meetings, they feel pointless." As Sammy listened, she saw a small door open. This could be the right time to ask Chao how his own absence and attitude might be contributing to the team breakdown and what he might do to help her with the team and get everyone back on track to making bonuses.

Sammy didn't pounce with her "fixes," nor did she start *shoulding on* him. Instead, she stayed curious and used the three options technique. After thanking him for sharing, she said, "Sounds like you and I have a shared goal, making our bonus. I also hear that you want to work in a place where it feels like a team and not dysfunction. May I offer some possible options that I see going forward? And, please know that I'm not tied to any of them. They're just ideas."

Chao said, "Go for it!"

Sammy offered the first option, for Chao to change nothing and continue fighting to make sales on his own without the team. Sammy set this up beautifully, "We always have the choice, and it is a choice to continue what we are doing even when it isn't working."

Chao responded, "I'd like to stop this headache and earn a bonus. So, no thanks. Next."

Sammy: "What would it look like if we took a day to meet as a team, outside the office, and spent time figuring out a structure that will better enhance our pipeline and how we leverage each other's networks?"

Chao became curious and said, "As long as we don't waste time and actually accomplish something. Let me consider that."

Sammy said, "Great. Just an option. I don't want to waste time either. I do think it's valuable though that we spend quality time with each other outside the weekly meeting. And beyond strategizing and building a better pipeline structure, we could consider getting to know each other better so that we have better relationships in general. You're the team rockstar, Chao. We look up to you and your high energy motivates us—and gives us new ideas to try in our own sales tactics. I'd love to see *that* Chao again, so what else might be a way that would help shift your frustration?"

Chao was quiet for a good two minutes as he ate. Sammy reported that she was literally biting her tongue to stay quiet. Then he said calmly, "Remember when the team used to go out for monthly beers? I miss that. It's been a long time since I knew what was going on with anyone at the office. And I think it is time we have a conversation with Paul. I've been tiptoeing around it, and it is time. Why don't you and I propose a one-day retreat with a structured agenda with Paul, then we go out for beers after?"

Sammy stayed silent for eight seconds. She didn't elaborate on Chao's third choice. She didn't gush over his change in attitude. She simply said, "Chao, I'm here to help, dude. Let's do it."

Remember, everyone likes to feel in control of their options, choices, and ultimate future. Our brain and mind take comfort when we have the freedom to choose what's right for us. Help wayfind with another to give their brain and mind that same sense of authorship!

PATH 3: CREATE CONDITIONS FOR COMMUNICATION SUCCESS

The speaker has shared something illuminating and you understand, value, and/or respect them better with your new insights. You feel that the gap between you is lessening. You wish you had a way to keep this communicative energy alive so as to not run into breakdowns in the future. You propose coming up with a clear structure, with their buy-in and engagement, to help you both communicate across any future gaps so that any breakdown can become a breakthrough.

We're back with Cass and Antony of the boba tea shops from the last chapter. Cass has been the senior manager of the stores for so long that she isn't used to having a thought partner to comanage and lead the team. It's hard to have two "cooks in the kitchen." Cass decides to take this path over coauthoring three options, focusing on how they will reconfigure the training program's playbook. She wants to ensure they can work together as a "two-headed manager" and be in sync with each of their individual communication needs.

We asked Cass how it went.

> After I said thanks for sharing, Antony. I appreciate you. I trust and respect your point of view and am looking forward to being a better comanager with you. May I propose that we go back to the office and come up with some ways that we can communicate better in the future

so that we can avoid pissing each other off? Maybe we can make our playbook of how we'll collaborate together? Because it really resonated with me when you said that you wanted me to call you out. I want you to feel comfortable calling me out, too. And I know that our staff and team would like it if we were aligned in how we manage them, together. Nobody wants to work for a two-headed monster. He quickly agreed and instead of coming up with our ideas on the drive back from our walk, I stayed in curiosity mode and learned all kinds of things about his family and upbringing. He's such an interesting dude. He's great. The perfect person for corporate to partner with me. I get it now.

That's great to hear, Cass! When you got back to the office, tell us about what happened and what you landed on.

It was easy. Many of the ones that you presented during the workshop I used, or we came up with our own version. I wrote on the board "Cass and Antony's Playbook: Conditions for Our Success" and offered the first condition, which was "Come to me in twelve hours if you feel that we've had a miscommunication or breakdown." I asked him how he felt about that.

He said, "Can you give me twenty-four hours? That works better for me given all that we juggle, plus I like reflection to ensure that I really am having an issue because sometimes it passes."

I said, "Sounds good," and changed it to The 24-Hour Rule. "Do you have one?"

He offered: "Please know that I'm only trying to do good by the tea shops and our staff and I'll do the same for you."

I wrote Assume Positive Intent on the board and asked if that sums it up for him. He agreed. We moved on and I added, "If you hear me giving a story that sounds untrue to you, ask me about it. Sometimes I can make mountains out of molehills in my head."

He laughed, "Oh, me too!"

I said, "OK, what about making this one called No Believing Stories We Made Up Inside Our Heads.

Then he said, "What about when we get really angry with each other? I don't handle conflict well—I tend to hide. Should we add that nothing is off limits to discuss if it helps make the stores better and our jobs easier?"

"Love that! Could we call it Practice Curiosity over Criticism? One of the things I'm learning is how to disrupt my reactions and get curious about why I'm feeling a certain way and then seeking out the others' perspective before I make assumptions and judgments. Another thing I'm learning is that this work is challenging and with everything going on it's easy to forget the agreements. I want them to work, so could we set aside the fifteen minutes during our Monday morning meeting to check in with these conditions to ensure that we're good and things are working—and just check in with each other about how we're feeling in general?"

"Yea, I'd like not to forget—keep us sharp. And I do think it's helpful to check in with each other in case something is going on in our personal life that is affecting our work performance. Good idea." He said.

I wrote Monday Morning Check-In.

Wow! Cass (and Antony) did a fabulous job. Cass carefully turned a breakdown with Antony into a clear breakthrough.

➤ The Big Aha! ◄

Creating clarity and structure about your communication strategies to prevent breakdowns from happening will make your relationship more successful. Writing it down will hold you both more capable and accountable to the agreements. Refer to it regularly and see it as an organic document, one that can grow and shift as your relationship expands. Being this transparent creates the conditions for success and provides grounding and context for how both of you can choose to behave when pressure strikes and hijacks either of you.

PATH 4: OFFER AUTHENTIC FEEDBACK

You're in a leadership role and have some influence over someone in your office. How you converse with them is a little bit different from most work relationships because what you say has power, impacting their output, evaluation, and employment. This path is tricky, because as we learned in Chapter 6, curiosity is a slippery slope, with curiosity fraud a constant danger—and this is a moment where you could breach any trust and respect you've fostered during the first half of the Curious Conversation. Remember that a true Curious Conversation isn't about *your* agenda. And in giving feedback, you always have an agenda.

Let's begin with what *not* to do.

Your Val's manager at a company that handles big corporate events and conferences. As a manager, you were trained in a strategy that, we believe, is a lazy way to give constructive feedback. See if you recognize this bullshit sandwich recipe:

Bottom bun: Give praise.

> Thanks for meeting me, Val. I truly enjoyed working with you on the Tamryn account. The way you handled admin on the timeline and project goals was terrific.

The meat: Pile on feedback and criticism.

> I noticed several times throughout, though, that you pushed the team on tasks that weren't of the utmost priority. I know that Marcus felt hammered by the deluge of texts and emails that you sent about updating files that weren't necessary—like receipts, and such. Patrice and Barbara also expressed to me that they felt pressured by you . . . and one even said that you texted her at 9 p.m. I don't really understand what you were thinking, but several times you sent me the same message via text message and email. I don't need double reminders like that. So, next time, please simmer down the amount of messaging about the deadlines. We know deadlines and tasks are important and we really were doing our best to keep up. But you stressed us out during a time when we didn't need more stress.

Top bun: Top it off with praise.

> Again, you did a phenomenal job keeping us all on task to meet our deadlines. We really couldn't have done it without you. Thanks, Val.

Poor Val! He was criticized for the very thing he was praised for in this bullshit sandwich. Most people know when they're being served one, so let's take these sandwiches off the menu. That feedback formula does little to bridge the gap, and potentially widens the expanse because this sandwich is full of passive-aggressive energy.

Let's say that you, as Val's manager, decide to lead with a Curious Conversation and ask: "*Val, may I offer you some feedback about the Tamryn account? I heard in our conversation that you're really good at keeping people on task and meeting deadlines. However, ...*" See how the same bullshit sandwich recipe emerges?

What will you do?

Giving feedback as a boss in this part of a curious conversation is tricky. We prefer using Path 2: Coauthor Three Options. But before we show you what to say to Val and how to say it, let's pause and see how our friend, expert leadership coach Susan Frazier, learned how to empower and support an employee better after choosing curiosity over criticism.

Dear Reader,

Like any longtime leader I have plenty of "war stories" to share. But over time most fade in importance or run together, as tried and true skills get honed. What does stick with you are the turning points, the firsts. Those moments when a "new to you" approach is risked, and your trajectory is forever changed.

That is the essence of my story with Paula. Although it was early in my career, I had responsibilities over both administrative and operations employees spread out over three locations. Paula worked in one of the centers, a 20-minute drive from my office at corporate. And she was a constant thorn. The employee that seemed to thrive on trouble. Since she was in the union, I could not just do the easy thing and let her go, the process was long and, at this company, seldom successful.

After a string of messy problems, Paula and I sat down one day and agreed to a set of rules she would play by. In that meeting I talked a lot. About why what she did mattered, about consequences to the company, and about potential actions I might be forced to take if she failed to change. Her usual defensive stance was gone that day, replaced by seemingly sincere regret. She seemed ready for change. In my mind I was doing my job, leading by explaining, and I silently patted myself on the back for being kind. I was only implicitly criticizing, no overt attacks because I was sure she just didn't understand how she was showing up.

Two days later she not just repeated, but escalated, the problem behavior. I was livid. I got in my car to make the 20-minute drive, fuming, plotting my equally escalated response. Halfway there I pulled over.

To this day I can't say where the thought came from, but I suddenly asked myself this question: What do I want? What is the very best outcome from this conversation with Paula? As much as I wanted the answer to be that she was wrong and I was right, the real answer was that I wished she would use her very clear skills for good instead of sabotage; that she would become an asset. That made me curious. What was going on? How could she seem so sincere one day and then mess up so soon after? As I sat in my car I formulated questions, ones I hoped would help her open up.

And open up she did.

I left that tearful conversation shaken. The circumstances of her life were beyond difficult and went most of the way to explaining her behavior. The rest of it, something I knew about personally, was crippling self-doubt that leads to self-sabotage. The difference between us was that I had found people who believed in me, helped me overcome, where she had the opposite—people close to her were telling her she was worthless.

I did three things that changed everything for Paula. The first was giving her a flexible schedule which helped with her personal situation. The second was to find her the right mentor. The third, and perhaps most impactful, I gave her more responsibility; I showed her that I trusted her, and she thrived.

Curiosity became an arrow in my leadership quiver that day, a tool that saved me again and again. Each time I felt anger, like I was right and others wrong, I took myself back to that day on the side of the road. It has served me well as a leader, but more importantly, as a human being. Paula, and her story, made me a better person.

With you,

Susan Frazier

Susan nailed it.

One of the key takeaways from Susan's letter is when she pauses to ask "What do I want? What is the best outcome from this conversation with Paula?" Susan situated herself in curiosity, suspending her need to be right, and used wayfinding to do three important things that would help Paula be successful.

Let's return to poor Val. What feedback could you give to him? Here's what to do:

"Val, thank you for telling me about your experience in managing the timeline and SMART Goals for the Tamryn account. I was hoping to understand better why it felt like—to me at least—that you were anxious about our team meeting the deadlines. You shined a light on that for me. Thank you. May I go through some feedback I received about how you handled your responsibilities?"

In this first part there is no overt praise, which will help make your next point stronger and clearer because there's no confusion over *am I being praised or criticized*?

Val says, "Sure! I probably stressed some people out."

"You did. And that's OK! We can improve upon on that in a moment. Thanks for being candid. I heard from three team members that they felt under pressure by the complexity of the project overall and when some of your reminders came through on text or after work hours, they felt it was excessive and adding to the pressure they already felt. I also received some of those reminders, and when they came two to four times in one day, it felt repetitive, and I became a little bit annoyed, too. Do you understand?"

Val nods.

In this part, you've succinctly laid out the feedback with context about the nature of the job itself (pressure) and how it personally impacted you. Asking Val if he understands allows him to clarify, rebut, and/or explain what he thinks and/or heard.

"I must hand you credit because you did accomplish your task—we met the deadline and the Tamryns are pleased clients. Next time, how might you hone your skills in managing the timeline for the team? May I offer the first option that I see?"

In this part, you offered praise—not with colorful adjectives or hype. Then you shifted to the coauthoring three options path (Path 2). You'll lay out the first option you've crafted as a viable solution for him to consider. You'll offer the next option to him and follow it with a third. At the end, you'll finish with gratitude.

"Thank you, Val, for hearing me today and sharing your thoughts and options. I look forward to the next project with you and supporting you as you grow on the team!"

PATH 5: A CURIOUS CONVERSATION IS COMPLETE. NOTHING TO ADD.

There are times when the experience of a curious conversation feels complete. The situation may be closed after you understand someone's perspective better. You value what you heard, and you can see how clean, curious listening and invitational language has amped up the level of understanding, trust, respect, and care in your relationship. There's really nothing more to say or do. The magic of *Tell me about* has helped bridged the gap.

This happened to Anne, the VP of Marketing of the pharmaceutical company from Chapter 1, after she had a series of

Curious Conversations with Dr. Malcolm, the chemical engineering "genius" behind the life-saving heart medication. These two experts needed to collaborate across the gap to successfully launch a drug that took nearly a decade to bring to fruition. Remember that Anne was struggling to understand his scientific data, vocabulary, and thinking. She disliked him, too, finding herself constantly annoyed by his negativity and naysaying about any of the campaigns her team proposed. According to her, he was always "throwing wrenches" in their best, well-articulated plans. However, without his approval their boss wouldn't sign off on the multipronged campaign. And poor Anne! Their boss revered "magical" Dr. Malcolm, insisting that if "Anne could just get along better with him, she'd be successful at her job." So, when Dr. Malcolm told their boss that she was often snippy and impatient with him in their interactions . . . it eroded any trust or respect Anne had left for him.

Anne was able to enter a series of Curious Conversations with Dr. Malcolm, leaning hard into suspending herself and leading with his preference to talk in "competent" terms about the medication. She listened closely for energy words and stayed in curiosity, gathering what she needed for her team to launch a successful campaign that he could support and the boss could sign off on.

Anne admitted to us several times that operating with that much self-awareness and personal responsibility was exhausting. However, she worked through it, and four separate two-hour-long curious conversations (that she intentionally held in his lab across a span of a week) gave her what she needed to bridge the gap and launch the campaign.

We asked her, "Did you consider using any of the other pathways, like coauthoring options or creating conditions for how you'll communicate better, together? Did you approach him about how it felt when he told your boss that you were snippy and impatient?"

In a nutshell, her response was,

"No. I didn't have time to work through options with him given the deadlines my team and I were facing. Plus, my boss didn't support me, and I don't think a person like Dr. Malcolm cares much about communicating across the gap. He's very much himself. He's an intelligent man who lives and breathes his work inside his lab."

This is a good path to take if you feel, like Anne did, that there is no point in the other pathways. Anne felt that her boss didn't get her perspective given his bias toward Dr. Malcolm, and Dr. Malcolm wasn't going to communicate across the gap fast enough to get the launch done.

We asked her, "Do you feel like you understand, like, and respect him now? Because when we met you, you were done. Fed up. Ready to quit—and what a disaster that would have been, delaying the launch of a medication that can save hundreds of thousands of lives."

Her answer: "If I'm being honest, he's not my cup of tea. I understand him as much as I can understand a chemical engineer who lives his life in a lab and breathes data. However, I was able to shift my kaleidoscope to see him as a fellow creative—and being in his lab, on his turf, helped me make connections that I had failed to see or hear by sequestering our interactions to the conference room. As for respect, I respect that he came up with this amazing medication and worked so hard on it for a decade because I certainly don't have that kind of tenacity or skills."

What we hear in her response is success!

The reality is that you may not fully understand, like, and respect the other after using the tools in this book. Rarely do we get the "whole enchilada" in life though, right? If you bridge two out of three, you're scoring high! If you bridge one out of three, you'll at least be able to collaborate effectively to do your job.

CRITICAL LAST THOUGHTS ON WAYFINDING AND CURIOUS CONVERSATIONS

You've now read several different ways a Curious Conversation and wayfinding can work to increase understanding, acceptance, and respect to bridge the gap and improve your connection, communication, and collaboration.

Please try to remember this: *Whether or not you're using words, you're always in a pseudo-conversation with someone—especially when you're stuck in the finger trap with them. You're always exchanging energy, even when words aren't present.* In this way, a Curious Conversation doesn't begin when you ask *Tell me about.* Curious Conversations truly begin when you take personal responsibility to show up clean and curious. Being an Explorer who moves toward the other in the relationship can shift many things from a negative to a positive in your dynamic. Also stepping into the Wayfinder role can dramatically increase positive outcomes simply by operating in service to the relationship—not just your agenda. Wayfinding helps us gain clarity about what we share back, our options, setting conditions for success, and how we give feedback.

Practice and have confidence in your new skills. Lead with curiosity and care—and you'll succeed.

REFLECTION QUESTIONS

- What would it feel like to be asked how another person can show up for you?
- Think about the array of one, two, or three options. Which of them makes your brain and mind feel the most supported?
- When was the last time you coached, mentored, or advised someone? What was that process like? How did that person react—would any of the approaches in this chapter have helped provide a more streamlined, clear path forward?

ACTION ITEM
The Choice: Wayfinding Over Would, Should, Could

Next time you feel a tug to offer advice, take a deep breath and ask how you can show up for the person you are in front of. Then, follow the other person's lead and support them with one of the paths.

JOIN THE CONVERSATION AND INTERACT ONLINE

#howyoushowupmatters

WHAT TO SAY AND HOW TO SAY IT
Language for Pressure-Based Moments

Things in life and at work get sticky and mucky.

Bridging the gap takes effort.

With all the education, strategy, and tactics we have offered you so far, you might still be thinking, *Sure, that works in theory, but what about all the high-pressure situations that are challenging?* You may be thinking, *I'm not good at thinking fast enough on my feet. I fumble and stumble to find words, ask questions, and reply with responsible language!*

To that end, below are some common situations where our clients have said, "Help! I'm under pressure! What can I say?"

The language below will help you find responsible ways to engage and move toward bridging the gap. We have chosen common pressure-based situations with some sentences, nuggets, phrases, and questions that you might choose to help you communicate most effectively.

TOP TEN PRO-COMMUNICATION REMINDERS

Before we release the language—i.e., "what to say and when to say it"—please remember that communication is much more than word selection. It is important to remember that your tone, approach, body language, and the context in which you use these starters is what makes all the difference.

Here are our tips to keep your gap bridging sharp and on point:

1. *Be brief and brilliant . . . then be gone.* Less is more. Overtalking can easily be a destroyer of connection. Extra words create added confusion. Finish a point, but don't hammer it into pulp. Simple words and sentence construction work best. When you are talking, try to come full circle, and put a simple bow on your thoughts.

2. *A smile goes a long way toward building connection and bridging gaps.* Keep your jaw loose and your shoulders relaxed.

3. *Focus on what you want to create more of.* If positivity is what you seek, then you must lead with positivity. If solution is what you seek, lead with solution-based questioning. Be the one who defies our current cultural need to talk about problems, gripes, and complaints rather than what's working well, solutions, or success. For example, try having Curious Conversations about another's success: be curious about how they achieved their goal and celebrate them!

4. *Don't interrupt. Period.* It is too easy to jump in and sling words that aren't necessary into the conversation. Hold tight. Wait. Enter the door into the conversation only when appropriate.

5. *Words hold power—they shape the files in your limbic system.* They are Ubuntu. So think about the "backstory" of meaning that comes with a word *before* you choose to utter it aloud. Use words that are responsible for the context, culture, and generation that you're working with.

6. *Never make a point without telling a short-story example.* And never tell that story without being clear on its point.

Too often, people start telling stories and never end up where they meant to go. Have a clear anchor in your story that can land well.

7. *Thinking and processing out loud often discredits you in relationships where you aren't close with the other person.* If you are looking to gain professional credibility, be sure to do your processing and thinking "off-line" before the conversation to bring your best, most confident and curious nuggets to the discussion.

8. *Silence is a secret weapon.* There is no reason you need to do all the talking and explaining. Hit pause. Let another person do the work. Silent equals listen.

9. *Practice humility, not cockiness.* Even if you know the answer, the path, and the solution—resist being a showoff. Humbleness in professional settings is attractive and powerful.

10. *Build more trust and respect by celebrating others—see others in complimentary ways that often go unnoticed.* Resist the urge to be an Eeyore, only paying lip service to what's crappy rather than flipping the script and celebrating what's worthy to note. Starting with what is going right with someone is a beautiful way to open a conversation.

PRESSURE SCENARIOS AND LANGUAGE STARTERS

Fundamentally, we prefer to open nearly all our Curious Conversations with some version of the *Tell me about* phrase. There are times, though, when it's obvious that phrase may not be appropriate for the moment. For instance, what if someone comes at you? What if the gap between you is quickly becoming a canyon and a more direct approach is needed? What if you need to be direct and curiosity won't work as the starting point?

The approaches we offer as ideas in this chapter are useful tools to have in your communication toolbox. Before taking them out for a spin, go to the bathroom and lock yourself inside. Practice saying the words to feel more comfortable using them in a variety of tones. You'll see quickly that if you attach the wrong tone, the language could backfire. So really watch yourself in the mirror and look at your facial expression. Listen to your tone. Find a few approaches that work for you and memorize them. Over time, they will naturally arrive when you need them most.

"Help! I'm under pressure! What can I say when I don't agree with the person in front of me?"

- "Tell me about what you are thinking. I am not sure I am on that same page."
- "I understand your point, and I am not on the same page. Could we get curious about where we might align?"
- "Could we explore another perspective? There may be more than one way to look at this."
- "I respect you and your point of view. I don't agree at this point. I am asking that we see how we might understand each other better by becoming curious about our differences."
- "That is one way to see it. And can we acknowledge that there are multiple ways to see the same issue?"
- "I am noticing a lot of speculation and interpretation going on here. Could we get back to some facts and try to understand each other in a new way?"
- "I respectfully disagree and want to find ways to bridge this gap. Can we ask someone to facilitate a conversation with us?"

"Help! I'm under pressure! What can I say when someone is constantly negative?"

- "Please share with me what has soured your perspective right now."
- "I hear you and understand that you feel upset. What do we need to do to turn this frustration into something that may help us in the future?"

- "How might I help with a change in perspective? I hear a lot of negatives and in my experience, solutions come when we move forward with positivity."
- "We are a team that focuses forward and keeps a positive tone. I need you to make a tone change if you plan to stay with us. Can we build a plan to help with that?"
- "Are you aware that the way you are communicating could be interpreted as hurtful or harmful? Are you intending this impact, or would you like to make a change?"
- "I'm feeling that things are getting a bit aggressive here, and that won't work for me/us. What can I do to help turn around the attitude?"
- "That kind of talk is making the problem bigger than it is: Would you please consider a change to your language?"
- "I am listening to your words, and they feel unconstructive. What can I do to help shift your energy?"
- "I am unclear about how your words are supportive right now. What can we do to help you say things differently?"

"Help! I'm under pressure! I messed up and need to make an apology and make it right."

- "I made a huge mess of things. I hope you can work to forgive me. I want to hear from you about how I can clean this up."
- "There's not a single excuse for what I did. I own it. Please forgive me. I am committed to making it right."
- "What I said was wrong/inappropriate. I own it. I am sorry."
- "I wish I could take it all back . . . and I can't. I feel terrible. I am here to listen to how it hurt you when you are ready and take responsibility in our relationship to make it better."
- "Clearly, I was beyond inappropriate. I was just plain wrong. Can we work together to clean this up?"
- "My actions were inexcusable. Please forgive the mess I have made. I want to make it right."

- "Even though I am sorry, I know it won't simply go away. I am here to work through it, and together if you'll allow me."
- "I never ever meant to hurt and disrespect you. I am so sorry."

"Help! I'm under pressure! What can I say when someone seems to be itching for a fight?"

- "Tell me about what has you coming at me this way?"
- "I am so sorry—I certainly didn't mean to offend you!"
- "I am so sorry we are in different corners. My desire is to build connection and understanding with you."
- "You seem really upset. What can I do to help understand the situation better?"
- "Can we attempt to keep this focused on the issue and not get so personal?"
- "Can we keep this professionally focused?"
- "There is still time for us to understand each other and work together."
- "I want to understand your frustration and anger. Can I please ask you to slow down so I can hear what this is about?"
- "I am willing—and desiring—to understand and resolve our past issues. Can we explore what that might look like?"
- "I feel your irritation and want to understand you better. I truly want to bridge the gap between us. Can we both commit to understanding each other?"

"Help! I'm under pressure! What can I say to refocus a conversation that has gone off the rails or sideways?"

- "I hear your perspective, and can we stay on track with this topic specifically?"
- "I am all for new ideas, and can we keep on this topic, please, before entertaining them?"

- "Let's stay focused on this right now."
- "I hear your desire to move the conversation this way, and let's stay focused for now on this topic."
- "I love where you are going and let's nail this part down first."
- "Your points are strong and let's not get lost down this rabbit hole."
- "I think we are getting distracted from the main point here."
- "Let's remember—this specific meeting/conversation is about [XXX]."
- "The core function of why we are here is to focus on is [XXX]. What am I not understanding in the linkage between that idea and this one? Please help me see it better."

"Help! I'm under pressure! What can I say to someone I have had a rift or disconnection or falling-out with?"

- "I know there has been tension. I am sorry about my part in it. Would you be open to having a conversation?"
- "I am so sorry for the distance between us. It was not my intention. I want to explore what we can do to better understand each other."
- "I feel like you and I got lost in our relationship. I would love to bridge the gap between us."
- "I would love to reconcile and take responsibility for my part in our distance. Would you be open to connecting?"
- "I want to restore our relationship. I want to bridge the gap between us. Can we connect and understand what it would take to move our relationship forward?"
- "I miss our relationship. Can we find a time to talk and understand each other again?"

"Help! I'm under pressure! What can I say to support an underperforming employee?"

- "Tell me about what you feel you are doing well and what you could be doing better?"
- "What distractions are taking you away from focusing on work right now? What do you need to change to get peak performance?"
- "Tell me about how full your plate is right now. Maybe I can help?"
- "Do we need to take a pause and regroup?"
- "This kind of underperformance isn't your norm. What is happening and how can we shift your performance?"
- "I know you are talented in your role, and I am not seeing that strength play out. How can we rebuild your strength?"

"Help! I'm under pressure! What can I say to help calm down a tense situation?"

- "I am sorry and can see that we just aren't understanding one another. We don't have to see eye-to-eye and in this company, we speak respectfully no matter what."
- "Maybe we can hit pause and reconvene when we all have taken a breath?"
- "You might want to argue, but I am not a fan. Could we find a different approach on this issue?"
- "This discussion is important and interesting and maybe we could learn more if our emotions were calmer. Shall we take a break?"
- "I don't know about you, but I need to cool my jets . . . . Shall we get back to this later?"
- "Being combative will take us nowhere. We are better than this. Let's regroup when we are calmer."
- "We are here to collaborate, not to tear each other down. I'm going to stop and remember who you are/who I am/who we are."

"Help! I'm under pressure! How can I say 'no' to a superior or my boss?"

- "My plate is full. What is most important to accomplish because I can't do everything?"
- "I need to say 'no' because that isn't in my job description, unless there was a change that I am not aware of."
- "I am OK to say 'yes' but that means I am saying 'no' to other things. Please understand I will not be able to complete my other tasks."
- "I am completely at my limit. Is this important enough to take me away from my core responsibilities?"
- "I wish I could divide myself. I cannot, so I need to say 'no' this time."
- "I want to play for this team, and yet I cannot see how this request is responsible or reasonable for the current situation."

"Help! I'm under pressure! How can I offer advice when I see a problem?"

- "I know you have thought this through, and can I offer an outsider's (or another) perspective?"
- "I am just wondering about your willingness for me to speak frankly about what I am seeing. I truly don't want to offend or sideswipe you. What works for you? What kind of feedback do you seek?"
- "Do you mind if I offer a suggestion?"
- "I want to throw out an idea and am wondering how willing your ears are to hearing one right now?"
- "You have done your homework and know a lot about this and is there an opening for me to suggest another idea?"
- "How can I show up for you right now? What's helpful? My ideas, frank opinion, or processing and listening with you?"

"Help! I'm under pressure! What can I say to my spouse/partner who is angry because of my work (and I genuinely want to repair it)?"

- "I am so sorry." (Pause . . . be with that person.)
- "I can see your day was long and hard. I am here now. What can I do to help?"
- "I was irresponsible and didn't communicate to you. That is on me. I am sorry." (Pause.)
- "I am so sorry. It looks like you've had a full day, too. I take full responsibility for not communicating better. Where did I drop the ball so that we can find a better solution moving forward?"
- "I love you. I messed up. I want to make it right." (Listen.)
- "Even though I am sorry, I know that doesn't make things right or go away. I am here to work through it with you."

"Help! I'm under pressure and I need to instill confidence in another."

- "You are so solid at what you do! You are golden!"
- "I love partnering with you—we make magic happen together!"
- "You are a total reliable partner—thanks for all your discipline!"
- "I have complete confidence in your talents and skills!"
- "Is there anything you can't do?!?! I love watching you kick butt!"
- "You are among the best workers here!"
- "Your ability to get stuff done is top-notch!"
- "I have 100 percent confidence in your ability and contribution!"

"Help! I'm under pressure and I want to celebrate and/or acknowledge another!"

- "I am very grateful for what [be specific] you have accomplished!"
- "Thank you for your contribution!"
- "How hard you are working is a true gift—thank you!"
- "Without your contribution, our achievement would not be so outstanding."
- "You rock!"
- "I owe you one. And I mean it—this mattered and you matter!"
- "I admire you and am better with you on my team. Thank you!"
- "Your commitment to excellence is a rarity—it matters. Thank you!"
- "I see you, all the ways you [be specific]. Thanks for showing up with your strengths and talents."

Again, practice this language in the mirror—say these words out loud, not only in your mind. Your tone, posture, face, and energy speak louder than words. Be responsible for how you show up—always emote warmth, conciseness, and curiosity, and always lead with a hope of bridging the gap.

REFLECTION QUESTIONS

- What language do you usually use to handle conflict?
- How do you celebrate people?
- Under pressure, what language do you default to and needs some maturing to keep up with your new communication skills?

ACTION ITEM

Identify a relationship where you may need a more direct approach. Learn a few key words or phrases from this chapter and practice saying them in private to ensure your tone and nonverbals are congruent. Then make the phrases your own so that you feel comfortable using them when necessary.

JOIN THE CONVERSATION AND INTERACT ONLINE

#useyourwords

TRAVERSING THE HARD STUFF
Gaps and Canyons

Communication is a messy business. From blasting zingers to poking bears, from healing wounds to clearing up misunderstandings, words can create both beauty and disaster. Whether we're on the giving or receiving end—nobody knows how their words will land. Even the best communicators and connectors struggle and fail, even when they show up with the best of intentions. Any conversation can possibly go sideways, up or down, even when you show up clean, curious, and use the tools.

The question is what do you do in your relationships when words are irresponsible and it doesn't feel like a gap you can bridge? How do you close what feels like an enormous distance between you and another? Time is of the essence because the longer the situation goes untouched, the more the gap widens and becomes a treacherous canyon. When emotions are high and time goes by, it's easy for the Inner Narrator to create a story that keeps you stuck in the finger trap. Hoping or waiting for someone else to initiate a resolution is an easy way to become frustrated, depressed, and apathetic. Someone needs to step up as the leader in the relationship.

You have options:

1. Do nothing. Duck out and disappear. Tolerate and ignore.
2. Play pretend that it's gone and fake it in the relationship.
3. Show up and try to bridge the gap, even when it feels like a canyon.

The brave choice is number 3, especially if you can choose to show up with an intention to care and your authentic self. Whether or not you were harmed, or your words harmed another, as a leader in your relationships it's your personal responsibility to close whatever distance you can despite any pain that you may feel. The good news is that, when carefully managed, breakdowns can create massive breakthroughs.

In the last chapter, we gave you direct language to use and mold for various situations where a more direct approach is required. Let's explore some common situations of various difficulty that show up in the workplace. In these scenarios, you can lead with the *Tell me about* invitation, or make a direct ask to see if there is a way you can clean up, heal, and/or repair any damage that was done.

WHEN YOU ARE HURT OR CONFUSED

Your darn human suit is sensitive. You get your feelings hurt, become confused by someone's behavior or attitude, and fall into a breakdown. You will be met with impasses, miscommunication about your opinions, and hardened perspectives. The pain point could be between you and a colleague that you trust and respect. The pain point could arrive when situations scale into ugliness. Either way, it's time to explore . . .

The Pain Point: Gossip, Breach of Trust.

Juan and Bill had worked together for nine years, and their families were close. Their kids had play dates, camped together, and played on the softball team, together. When Juan returned to the office after a late lunch, he heard Bill in the breakroom and his jaw dropped. Bill was gossiping about Juan and his home life, sharing completely inappropriate and private details to their fellow coworker. Juan felt like he was being thrown under the bus, especially when Bill talked about their night of drinking a couple weeks ago. For the next five minutes, Juan stood outside the door listening. He couldn't believe it! How in the world could he confront Bill about the crap he just heard come out of his mouth? Juan walked away and took a deep breath. An hour later, he called Bill for a conversation.

The Pain Point: They Rejected Me.

Arlene, our friend from the home-based business in Chapter 7, who struggled with passive, pleaser listening, has decided to speak with the representatives that have formed their new group. Arlene understands how the global pandemic, divisive election, and mask mandates drove them to cleave off from the entire group. She doesn't agree with their decision, and she accepts it—she has let go of any need to change their minds and bring them back into the fold of the team. She also feels ashamed that she wasn't able to keep her group cohesive under her leadership despite obstacles that were out of her control. Her hurt still remains when she thinks about the new group. She can't help but feeling that there is lingering negative energy between them. She decides to clean it up between her and them to keep their working relationship strong.

The Pain Point: They Devalue Me.

Bao feels disrespected by Marlene, a senior associate in their office who often dismisses her ideas as immature, unpolished, and "just not there yet, honey." Bao has yet to hear a positive, affirming thing about her work from Marlene. She respects Marlene, and that's part of the problem—when Marlene behaves like this Bao feels worthless. She feels like she'll never live up to Marlene's way of doing things. While Bao understands that she has more growth and learning in her career, she doesn't know how much longer she can stand to have every idea shot down. When Marlene calls her "honey," it feels disingenuous and like being a served bullshit sandwich. There is stuck energy and Bao decides to take action and talk to Marlene.

The Pain Point: I Have No Idea What Happened.

A colleague hasn't looked you in the eyes for weeks. Whenever you enter a room where they are, they leave and don't acknowledge you. What is going on? Did you do something wrong? Why are they avoiding you?

Any of these examples feel familiar? Here's a process that helps to clear up the pain point hurt, misunderstanding, and stuck energy.

Steps in the Process

1. You have the courage and willingness to address this with the other person. You say, "Would you be open to clearing something up with me? I feel there's been a misunderstanding/breakdown in our relationship."
2. They can respond with either "Yes" or "No":
   a. A *YES* response signifies that the listener believes he or she is ready. Watch for clues in their response and body language that may suggest otherwise. If you intuit that they truly aren't ready to clear this up, back off a bit and begin a Curious Conversation and see where it goes.
   b. A *NO* response signifies that the listener is resistant. Perhaps the listener isn't in the right space or doesn't have the proper time available. Ask if you can agree to a future time for the process to occur. Be prepared to offer times and dates that work for you.
3. If they respond with YES, then share your issue according to the following process with care and curiosity:
   a. Cite a *specific example* that sparked the breakdown/disconnect/hurt/wound. Avoid entirely generalities like "you always" or "you never." Name your pain: hurt, frustrated, irritated, angry . . .
   b. State the *facts* of the interaction. Facts are undisputed things that actually occurred, were mutually observed, and/or agreed upon by both parties. If there are no facts, don't make up any.

    c. Share what personal responsibility you own in the situation. Do your best to not to place blame on the listener.

4. If they interject and become defensive, allow them to spill their very full human cup. Don't bite on their words. Control your face and body reactions. Don't cross your arms. Remain open, curious.

5. When they finish, take a moment to reflect back to them what you heard, including what happened, how it made them feel, and the meaning that you applied to the situation. If you can, show how you understand what happened with any new insights about why the pain point occurred. Please note that this does not constitute an agreement—or that you agree with what they've shared back. If appropriate, feel free to ask, "Does this sound correct to you?"

6. Once you believe that the listener fully understands the situation and what it was like for you, say, "Thank you for listening. I value our relationship and want it to be as strong as can be. Thank you for clearing this up with me."

Overall, this process is not for the faint of heart. It is for brave humans who want to bridge the gap and not let it grow into a canyon. Use this approach when you have a strong desire to move past the pain point and get a relationship back on track. Show up, make the ask, and let your care for this relationship guide you as you try to rebuild trust and respect.

YOUR GENUINE APOLOGY IS NEEDED

Andre had been working from home for the past year. He loved his newfound work-from-home lifestyle, even though he found himself slipping professionally. Last Friday, right after the morning team huddle, he decided to get in a run even though it was time for a client call that his boss wanted him to hear. He thought, I don't even need to mention it to anyone—how would they know? He grabbed his earphones, connected to the call, muted himself and turned off his video, and began his run. Somewhere along the way, his pocket unmuted him and his boss heard him heavy breathing . . . and then his bathroom break along the trail. His boss texted him, "Do you want to mute next time you flush the toilet? I can hear your breathing and it's distracting and inappropriate." Paul thinks, "Oh crap." Time to apologize for his irresponsibility.

Maria was sick to her stomach. She told her business partner Julia that she'd turn in the expense reports and make sure the numbers looked good to pass muster with their client. Maria and Julia had every intention of making the rest of their calls and completing the hours they billed by the end of the week. When the client called an hour later, pissed because they discovered that two of their contacts weren't ever reached—Maria panicked and blamed Julia. "Julia told me she made those calls. I'm so sorry. She's been under the gun lately with a cancer scare. I'll call them today. So sorry." The client responded with "Oh my god, what kind of cancer? I'll reach out to Julia." Not only did Maria fudge the reports, but she also threw Julia under the bus and then it spiraled. Julia didn't have a cancer scare . . . and now the client may say something. Time for both of them to come clean to both parties.

Joanne raced to her daughter's varsity soccer game. She was flustered after a long day at her dental practice. As she drove, she was trying to shake off her frustration at a patient who yelled at her. As she pulled up to the soccer field her daughter came running up to the car, crying, "How could you miss my game . . . you knew it was at 4 p.m., not 6 p.m.! We talked about it this morning! You were the only mom not there and the recruiters were watching today!"

You blew it.

You were selfish. You forgot. You stretched the truth. You lied. You threw them under the bus. You said something hurtful. You thrashed their values. You didn't listen. You made assumptions. You judged unfairly. You manipulated. You fell short. You overpromised. You gossiped. You ignored. You snubbed. You turned someone's words into weapons.

You were wrong.

Everyone has fallen short when it comes to integrity, causing harm to one another. An apology is about taking ownership over your actions and shortcomings. An apology is about clearing up a wrong and coming to terms with changing your behavior so as not to make the same mistake in the future.

Our secret is to apologize with hearty depth. Do not give a pithy, little *I am sorry*. Say it with bold honesty: *I own what I did and I'm sorry*. Here are some ways:

* *I'm sorry that I xxx. I take full responsibility for xxx.*
* *I'm sorry that I xxx. I know how I can avoid this in the future. I care about our relationship. Is there more you want to share about how it impacted you?*
* *I'm sorry for xxx. I truly hope you can hear me. I am learning. I am open to your help and wisdom on how I can show up and interact with you with better.*

When possible, stand in silence for eight seconds after you hear what they respond/react with. Allow the power of silence to convey that you heard, saw, and respected what they uttered. Always listen with clean ears—no interjections or defending what you did with why. Stay in the Circle of Choice even when you're inclination is to slide into the Drama Triangle. Don't over-apologize. Don't replay or rehash it out incessantly. Don't loop or talk in circles, remain in warm conciseness.

Then forgive yourself and move on. Release the pain and don't become trapped by it—learn and grow.

WHEN THEY STONEWALL YOU, REFUSE TO COMMUNICATE

You have all these tools to use now in your communication toolbox. You have the heart and energy to bridge the gap. You show up clean and curious. You try *Tell me about* . . .

Everything falls flat.

They ignore, are suspicious, or reject your efforts.

They tell you to mind your own business.

You're hurt. Disappointed. Flummoxed.

It is very possible you won't be able to bridge the gap with certain people. A great relationship often consists of two people who stand more on the side of readiness than in stubborn resistance. And because of our free agency, you cannot ever force someone into something when they're not ready to engage. How you respond to this resistance, suspiciousness, immaturity, and/or stubbornness is simple. Voice a willingness to back off and a commitment to being available when the time is right for them to bridge the gap. Don't allow any tone to enter your voice other than care and concern. It might sound like this:

- *I understand that you're not wanting to speak with me. I won't keep asking. And I'll always be here to walk through anything with you when you're ready to talk.*
- *Got it. I'll back down. I'm here if you ever want to discuss what's happened between us.*
- *I totally hear that you want me out of this. Consider it done. If you ever change your mind—I am here and look forward to closing this gap between us.*

Practice patience. Keep your word and keep showing up with clean and curious energy when you're around them.

WHEN YOUR VALUES ARE CROSSED

Do you see yourself in this example?

You've got fifteen minutes before the training begins and you're catching up on email, feeling like for once you have some semblance of control over your inbox from hell! It's been a long week—one more training to get through, then lunch, then home. Pat enters. She is a member of the admin support team. You're focused and jamming when Pat's voice grows louder and louder. She's talking fast and furious, all expletives and hyperbole. Words that have no place being voiced in this setting, nor in any that you can really think of. You shoot Pat your best glare. Albert walks over and distracts you, then the training starts.

It's lunch. You grab your phone and walk outside for thirty minutes to grab a sandwich. The fresh air feels so good and the sun on your back makes you smile. It is almost the weekend. You start scrolling and there's Pat again, going off online with utterly ridiculous and despicable posts.

Stop already, you scream to yourself. Yet there she goes again shaming and blaming an entire group of people for the woes of this country, railing against everything you hold to be true and fair in the world. The posts seem to strive to incite division and reaction. The memes and images on her feed turn your whole body rigid. You want to fight, and the feeling is visceral as you feel your fists close and clamp down on your phone. Enough is enough. Your values have been crossed. It's time to confront Pat.

You probably have been—or will be—in an interaction where outrageous, extreme thoughts are shared. Perhaps it is a conversation where racist, sexist, or other discriminatory language was spewed. Maybe the beliefs are so egregious and one-sided that you must stand up and say something.

Your values compel you to show up with courageous conviction and speak your nonnegotiables, setting perimeters about how others may engage with you. In these situations, we bring a clean tongue and a direct, fair presence to the situation. We speak about how our values are being crossed. We express what we will and will not allow.

In the moment, it is handy to have practiced a few sentence starters to help you articulate a response and avoid an explosive reaction. Here are a few ways to clearly stand in your values:

- *I disagree with xxx. One of my core values is xxx. For me that means xxx. I disagree with the lumping of all xxx people into a stereotype or simple category. If you want to hear my perspective further, I am happy to share some stories, and please know that this value of mine cannot be altered.*
- *I hear your words and the feeling inside of them. I don't see it that way. I don't share your perspective. My values say xxx, and that's why I operate with xxx.*
- *I disagree with you, but I appreciate the tension that it brings to our relationship, so I ask that we continue asking questions that hopefully will land us in a better place.*
- *This is very awkward and hard because I care about you. When your language and perspective are rooted in your false*

information, I cannot participate. If you want to explore a different story with me sometime, where we choose to be curious rather than certain, then I am all in.

Finally, we ask for a follow-up conversation to discuss it further when we can show up cleaner and more curious, and when our human cup is less full.

THE CANYON: WHEN AN IDENTITY IS NEGATED, ERASED, THRASHED

What do you do when the gap you experience is not something you can close on your own? What about when it truly becomes a treacherous canyon?

From harmful microaggressions to blatant discrimination—damage happens and canyons widen. You probably want to enlist professionals to help you traverse this rough landscape.

When these "earthquakes" shake us, it's time to pause and reflect about the contributing factors, and that usually means looking at how our values and beliefs rub against another's.

Your values are derived from your lived experiences and become beliefs that you hold tight. They are like your personal compass and become the standards by which you make decisions, structure your life, and build meaning. Your values can shift, mature, and even be discarded as you age and gain more lived experiences. Your values are jewels in your kaleidoscope, and it's worth being curious about which jewels are bigger than others, why, and how they contribute to your relationships. These big jewels color your unique perspective and are often inextricable from your core identity. In Chapter 9, we briefly touched upon them with the healthcare association. In Chapter 10, we illustrated them through Jackie's health consciousness.

Now, we ask you to think about the big jewels that pattern your world. One way to begin this self-exploration is to write down lived experiences that changed you, explore the repetitive stories that you tell yourself and others, reflect on what you read and listen to, and consider whom you surround yourself with.

How do all these things in your kaleidoscope overlap? What is the common denominator? What's essential for you to be who you are?

Your big jewels impact how you communicate at work and beyond, especially when it comes to discussions about:

- Race
- Gender
- Sexuality and family
- Economic class and stratification
- Religion and spiritual beliefs
- Politics and the role of government

When people fail to be curious about, acknowledge, and/or respect someone's values in these discussions, they negate someone's identity. This is like taking a giant eraser and rubbing it all over someone—doing away with what they don't want to see, hear, or acknowledge. It's saying, "*Your big jewel is not real. It doesn't exist in the pattern of life; therefore, you don't exist in the pattern of life.*" How incredibly frustrating and utterly destructive to hear that. Refuting, thrashing, arguing, or even joking about people's values creates canyons. Nobody feels understood, accepted, valued, or respected.

Often, people negate others' values because it has challenged something deep within them, whether they're conscious of it or not. Sometimes, people unintentionally negate others because of the Golden Rule—only wishing to see that which can be mirrored back to them. Talking about these big jewels—with anyone—is tough. And, at work in particular, we end up facing some of our most challenging conversations because we don't have friendship or love to keep us wholly engaged and moving forward. It's a minefield ripe for miscommunication and explosions.

Let's acknowledge it flat out—we are two upper-middle-class white women who are entrepreneurs working in Northern California and raising children. We cannot zip off our human suit. We cannot change the color our skin. We cannot escape our values, geography, and the season of life we find ourselves in. We, too, are doing the best we can given who we are. However, we can practice self-awareness, suspend ourselves, and be curious about how race, gender, sex, family, class, religion, politics, and geography shape our behavior, communication, and relationships. We can shift our kaleidoscope to see our own patterns and those of others. And it's absolutely possible to do it without being hijacked by the invisible forces, nor defaulting to reaction, defensiveness, and argumentation.

We'd also like to state that this book is not a DEI book (diversity, equity, and inclusion). There are many DEI experts to read and to hire to navigate this critical work of traversing the canyons of discrimination. As you, or your organization, look to grow and explore this type of work, we invite you to hire someone skilled in "DEIB" work, which includes the "B" for belonging.

In "belonging," people choose to accept the differences of people and care about their fellow human. In a polarizing world, too often people engage in "othering," which happens when one person/group doesn't see the other person/group as being "normal," and therefore shuns them in a myriad of ways. The Othering and Belonging Institute at UC Berkeley[1] has tools and research to help you understand DEIB work and its impact on your work and relationships.

➤ The Big Aha! ◄

For us, the truth remains that you can't be in a real, working collaborative relationship with anyone without practicing belonging. You work on a team, and as we stated in Chapter 1, you rarely get to choose who you work with, and you need diversity of thought and skills to accomplish your work. Being part of a team means that everyone belongs.

Our tools for showing up curious and clean are the perfect primer for DEIB work. We have tried to boil the gap between people down to its simplest form: closing the space between met and unmet emotional needs. By focusing on everyone's fundamental emotional need to be understood, accepted, and valued, we hope to not only bridge the gap between others but to also begin setting up the equipment needed to traverse these tough canyons and conversations.

As white women, we are doing our best to show up in perhaps the toughest, and most important, conversation that has many struggling in the finger trap: race. Our goal in this book, and in any Bridge the Gap experience, is to help everyone reach a state of belonging, where they can be seen and heard in meaningful ways that create a better team. In doing that, we acknowledge and uplift that representation and inclusivity of diverse people from all backgrounds and walks of life matter, in particular, people of color who have been historically harmed by structural and systemic inequities and injustices. And as representatives of red and blue, we are ready for a purple nation. We believe our tools can build a tribe of people who know how to communicate, collaborate, and connect across these treacherous divides.

We show up to these conversations as best we can, given the limitations of our human suit and the big jewels in our unique kaleidoscopes . . . even when it's uncomfortable, challenging, and people are throwing daggers. The best we can do is set up an environment where people can belong—where they come to know and care about one another through sharing their lived experiences and by twisting their kaleidoscopes.

LAST THOUGHTS

We believe that you can bridge the gap. We believe your professional relationships, and all your relationships, are worth learning these skills. We believe you can work in an environment where people communicate better and have more meaningful relationships. It takes a special kind of fortitude to look in the mirror and face our self and how we show up, speak, and engage with people who are different from us.

You've made it this far—keep going.

Together, we can bridge the gaps at work, in our families, and in our communities.

We thank you and we're with you.

REFLECTION QUESTIONS

- Was there a situation that you were involved in that was never cleared up? Did it blow over, or did the harm fester and manifest over time?
- What was the best apology you ever received? How did that person relay it to you?
- What was the worst apology you ever received?
- Remember a time when your values were thrashed . . . what ensued? Did you clean it up? Did you stand up for yourself (or others?)?

ACTION ITEM

The Choice: Communication Over Miscommunication

Practice apologizing in the mirror. Lock the bathroom door, turn the fan on so nobody can hear you. And apologize for something that you may have never cleaned up. Watch yourself in the mirror, listen to how you sound, feel it all, and practice.

JOIN THE CONVERSATION AND INTERACT ONLINE

#communicatebetter

TO BRIDGE OR NOT TO BRIDGE
Your Choice

Dear Reader,

Be curious about how you show up.
Be curious about being ready.
Be curious about how you react under pressure.
Be curious about how you think under pressure.
Be curious about the jewels in your kaleidoscope.
Be curious about the patterns in your stories.
Be curious about what makes you communicate best.
Be curious about disrupting your default behaviors.
Be curious about how people are different than you.
Be curious about how you show care.
Be curious about what makes people trust and respect you.
Be curious about how you lead and structure your
    conversations.
Be curious about language.
Be curious about energy.
Be curious about what's possible.
Be curious to bridge the gap.
We believe in you. We're here if you need us.

With you,

Jennifer and Katie

ACKNOWLEDGMENTS

Dear Readers,

A book or a business is never birthed alone. Thank you to our tribe of intellectuals, dreamers, strategists, and communicators for being with us on this journey! Thanks to our agent, William Gladstone of Waterside Productions, for taking a chance on us. We are forever grateful. Thank you to the entire team at McGraw Hill Professional: Amy Li, Donya Dickerson, Jonathan Sperling, and Scott Sewell. To our fierce and mighty editor, Ruth Mills, of Mills Literary Services, we adore you! Many thanks to Beth Baugher of True Love Photo for making us look and feel like superstars. Last, thanks to our brilliant team at Fortier Public Relations: Mark Fortier, Norbert Beatty, and Rebecca Proulx for working so hard to get our message of curiosity, connection, and collaboration out into the world. We are so grateful!

—Jennifer and Katie

From Jennifer:

I still am convincing myself that this work is finally a reality and being shared with the world.

I know I would not be here without a strong and faithful God, who has been my way-maker and my miracle worker. My family has taught me many of the greatest lessons, on a journey that has been unexpected and beautiful. To my daughters, Allison, Taylor, and Lauryn: I love you and I am beyond grateful God chose me to be your mother. Martin Menard: you are a bright blessing of love and adventure and a total gift in my life. Thank you to my parents Perry and Kathleen Edwards: you continue to raise us to be contributors in this world and you have showed us how to show up with our absolute best. Thank you to my Aunt Sal who lovingly kicked me in the butt so many times to get this book written: your encouragement and confidence has been a difference maker. To my home community of Placer County: thank you for being such a generous family of supporters for small business and entrepreneurs.

For the past 20 years, I have had the utter privilege of walking beside brilliant and caring humans, building meaningful businesses, and making remarkable impacts on the world. I may have been the "expert," but in my time with these people, they were also the teachers. While I can't name them all, I can thank each of them deeply for the love and partnership we experienced together—you have become like family. As iron sharpens iron, so one person sharpens another. I am beyond grateful for those who have sharpened me over the years. You are my chosen family—you know who you are. The encouragers, prayer warriors, and active friends who have challenged me: you have now pushed me to grow beyond what I had ever perceived as possible, and I thank you.

Love, Jennifer

From Katie:

I have so many people to thank for bringing me to this moment. To the most amazing human on the planet, Nicholas Miller, thank you for your love and belief. To our children, Cal and Kinsey, you've taught me more about curiosity, language, meaning, and connection than anyone or anything. To my mother and stepfather, Julia and Nigel Moore, for showing me what success looks and feels like. To my father and stepmother, Hamilton and Aladean McCleary, for keeping me grounded. To my sister, Kristie: squeak! To my chosen family, Cathie and Scott Fields, I love you like blood.

Writers and entrepreneurs are supported by a village of wisdom and strength. I am blessed to be surrounded by cheerleaders, mentors, and geniuses. Thank you to my wonderful tribe who keeps me laughing, learning, and growing—in particular: Desiree Bell Kiesel, Angela Caldwell, Stacey Powell, Susan Frazier, Garrett Berdan, Shane Logan, Dr. Michael Marion Jr., Janis Haag, Katie McConnell Olson, Mackenzie Weiser, Jeannie Howell, April Peletta, Laura Martin, Rachel Zillner, Christie Black Davis, Darcy Totten, Jasper James, Kari Shipman, Bethany Leach, Bonnie Ferreira, Kevin McCarthy of Change Rx, April Javist, Chris and Tara Baltzley, Andru Defeye, Maya Wallace, Paul Willis, Paulette Greenhouse, Rob Stewart, Krista Minard, Michael Spurgeon, Jean Fox, Stella Premo, Chris Worden, Marilyn Reynolds, Ed Cole, Kathy Les, Julie Woodside, Justin Self, Reverend Kevin Ross, Dr. Leonard Abbeduto, Daniel Kaufman, Jim Tabuchi, Barbara Modlin, Tamaira Sandifer, and my family at Mastermind, 916 Ink, CapRadio, the American Leadership Forum, Sacramento Splash, Studio T Arts and Entertainment, and Visions in Education.

And finally, much love to my beloved city of Sacramento and its residents—you've made my life simply the best.

I adore you all, Katie

NOTES

CHAPTER 1

1. Generational Differences in the Workplace [infographic], Purdue University, accessed December 28, 2020, https://www.purdueglobal.edu/education-partnerships/generational-workforce-differences-infographic/.
2. Ross Douthat, "10 Theses About Cancel Culture," *The New York Times,* July 14, 2020, https://www.nytimes.com/2020/07/14/opinion/cancel-culture-.html.
3. Bill Knaus, "It's Not What You Say—It's How You Say It!," *Psychology Today*, November 19, 2013, https://www.psychologytoday.com/us/blog/science-and-sensibility/201311/it-s-not-what-you-say-it-s-how-you-say-it.

CHAPTER 2

1. Alena Hall, "The Key to Happiness at Work That Has Nothing to do with Your Actual Job," *Huffington Post*, February 4, 2015, https://www.huffpost.com/entry/happiness-at-work_n_6613358.
2. Virgin Pulse, "Labor of Love: What Employees Love about Work and Ways to Keep the Spark Alive," *Virgin Pulse*, 2015, Accessed December 22, 2020, https://connect.virginpulse.com/files/Survey_LaborofLove.pdf.
3. Jessica Stillman, "A Review of 174 Studies Concluded This Is the Most Important Quality for Happy Relationships: It Improves Every Kind of Close Relationship and Yes, It Can Be Cultivated," *Inc.*, December, 29, 2020, https://www.inc.com/jessica-stillman/happiness-relationships-psychological-flexibility.html.
4. Neal Burton, "Our Hierarchy of Needs," *Psychology Today*, May 23, 2012, https://www.psychologytoday.com/us/blog/hide-and-seek/201205/our-hierarchy-needs.
5. Human Givens Publishing Limited, Brett Culham, "The Emotional Needs Scale," *Human Givens Journal*, Volume 15, No, 3 (2008): https://www.hgi.org.uk/resources/delve-our-extensive-library/resources-and-techniques/emotional-needs-scale.

6. "Jon Kabat-Zinn Quotes," *GoodReads*, accessed December 22, 2020, https://www.goodreads.com/author/quotes/8750.Jon_Kabat _Zinn.

7. Craig Freudenrich and Robynne Boyd, "How Your Brain Works," HowStuffWorks.com, June 6, 2001, https://science.howstuffworks .com/life/inside-the-mind/human-brain/brain8.htm.

8. Jerome Groopman, "Can Brain Science Help us Break Bad Habits?," *New Yorker*, October 21, 2019, https://www.newyorker.com /magazine/2019/10/28/can-brain-science-help-us-break-bad-habits.

9. Chris Bergstrom, "Mindfulness and the Brain Made Easy," Blissfulkids.com, December 11, 2017, https://blissfulkids.com /mindfulness-and-the-brain/.

10. Nancy Moyer, "Amygdala Hijack: When Emotion Takes Over," Healthline.com; April 22, 2019, https://www.healthline.com/health /stress/amygdala-hijack.

11. Jacquelyn Cafasso, "Chemical Imbalance in the Brain: What You Should Know," Healthline.com; December 4, 2019, https://www .healthline.com/health/chemical-imbalance-in-the-brain.

12. Elena Childers, "How Nostalgia Affects Your Brain," *Break Through Radio Today*, August 31, 2016.

13. Shintaro Funahashi and Jorge Mario Andreau, "Prefrontal Cortex and Neural Mechanisms of Executive Function," *Journal of Physiology-Paris*, Volume 107, Issue 6 (2013), pp. 471–482, http:// www.sciencedirect.com/science/article/pii/S0928425713000223.

14. Judith Glaser and Richard D. Glaser, "The Neurochemistry of Positive Conversations," *Harvard Business Review*, June 12, 2014, https:// hbr.org/2014/06/the-neurochemistry-of-positive-conversations.

15. The University of Queensland Australia, "The Limbic System," Accessed December 22, 2020, https://qbi.uq.edu.au/brain/brain -anatomy/limbic-system#:~:text=The%20limbic%20system%20is %20the,and%20fight%20or%20flight%20responses.

16. Bryan Kolb, and Gibb Robbin, "Brain plasticity and behaviour in the developing brain." *Journal of the Canadian Academy of Child and Adolescent Psychiatry* 20(4), 2011, pp. 265–76, https://www .ncbi.nlm.nih.gov/pmc/articles/PMC3222570/.

17. Courtney E. Ackerman, "What is Neuroplasticity, a Psychologist Explains," Positivepsychology.com, December 10, 2020, https:// positivepsychology.com/neuroplasticity/.

CHAPTER 3

1. Jason Castro, "Where Does Identity Come From?," *Scientific American*, May 28, 2013, https://www.scientificamerican.com /article/where-does-identity-come-from/.

2. Nathan Collins, "Stanford Researchers Explore How the Human Mind Shapes Reality," Stanford.edu *News*, June 11, 2018, https://news.stanford.edu/2018/06/11/four-ways-human-mind-shapes-reality/.

3. Carolyn Gregoir, "5 Amazing Things Your Brain Does While You Sleep," September 29, 2014, *Huffpost*, https://www.huffpost.com/entry/brain-sleep-_n_5863736.

4. Megan Holohan, "Some People Don't Talk to Themselves, Are They Better Off?" Today.com/Health, February 7, 2020, https://www.today.com/health/experts-talk-about-what-it-means-have-inner-monologue-t173490.

5. Russell T. Hurlburt, Christopher L. Heavey, Jason M. Kelsey, "Toward a Phenomenology of Inner Speaking, Consciousness and Cognition," *Science Direct* 22(4), 2013, pp. 1477–1494, https://www.sciencedirect.com/science/article/abs/pii/S1053810013001426?via%3Dihub.

6. Rebecca Gladding, "Don't Believe Everything You Think or Feel," June 21, 2011, *Psychology Today*, https://www.psychologytoday.com/us/blog/use-your-mind-change-your-brain/201106/don-t-believe-everything-you-think-or-feel.

CHAPTER 4

1. Homepage, "The Original Drama Triangle Article," Karpman DramaTriangle.com, Accessed December 30, 2020, https://karpmandramatriangle.com/.

CHAPTER 5

1. Matt Weber, Harvard Graduate School of Education EdCast, "Unlocking the Immunity to Change," March 10, 2014, https://www.gse.harvard.edu/news/14/03/harvard-edcast-unlocking-immunity-change.

2. James Nestor's book "Breath: The New Science of a Lost Art" provides a fascinating overview on the health benefits of breathing. His website (https://www.mrjamesnestor.com) provides information and videos.

3. Brigid Schulte, "Harvard Neuroscientist: Meditation Not Only Reduces Stress: Here's How it Changes your Brain," *Washington Post*, May 26, 2015, https://www.washingtonpost.com/news/inspired-life/wp/2015/05/26/harvard-neuroscientist-meditation-not-only-reduces-stress-it-literally-changes-your-brain/.

4. Marilyn Mitchell, "Dr. Herbert Benson's Relaxation Response: Learn to Counteract the Physiological Effects of Stress," *Psychology Today*, March 29, 2013, https://www.psychologytoday.com/us/blog/heart-and-soul-healing/201303/dr-herbert-benson-s-relaxation-response.

5. Bessel A. Van der Kolk, *The Body Keeps the Score: Brain, Mind, and Body in the Healing of Trauma,* Penguin Books, 2015.

6. All Things Considered, " 'Call Your Friends: The Importance of Maintaining Friendships During the Pandemic," *National Public Radio,* March 27, 2020, https://www.npr.org/2020/03/27/822728362/call-your-friends-the-importance-of-maintaining-friendships-during-the-pandemic.

7. James Pennebaker and Cindy Chung, "Expressive Writing, Emotional Upheavals, and Health," in *Foundations of Health Psychology,* Oxford University Press, 2007, https://www.researchgate.net/publication/253937612_Expressive_Writing_Emotional_Upheavals_and_Health. To get started with therapeutic free writing please consider Pat Schneider's seminal book: "Writing Alone and With Others," (Oxford University Press, 2003) and learn more about her life's work at www.amherstwriters.org.

8. Greater Good Science Center, "The Science of Gratitude" (whitepaper), University of California, Berkeley, May 2018, https://ggsc.berkeley.edu/images/uploads/GGSC-JTF_White_Paper-Gratitude-FINAL.pdf?_ga=2.116966406.122771174.1609457631-601148795.1609368105.

9. Harvard Health Publishing, "The Power of Forgiveness," Harvard Medical School (website), May 2019, https://www.health.harvard.edu/mind-and-mood/the-power-of-forgiveness.

10. Gabrielle Forleo, "Feel and Believe What You're Saying Is True with These Affirmations," Chopra.com, November 20, 2020, https://chopra.com/articles/feel-and-believe-what-youre-saying-is-true-with-these-affirmations.

11. Erica M. Jackson, "FACSM STRESS RELIEF: The Role of Exercise in Stress Management," *ACSM's Health & Fitness Journal* 17(3), May/June 2013, pp. 14–19, https://journals.lww.com/acsm-healthfitness/fulltext/2013/05000/stress_relief__the_role_of_exercise_in_stress.6.aspx.

CHAPTER 6

1. SHRM October 2019 Omnibus, "Politics in the Workplace Report," SHRM, November 5, 2019, https://www.shrm.org/about-shrm/press-room/press-releases/pages/survey-finds-alarming-rise-of-politics-at-work.aspx.

2. UCI News, "Awe Promotes Altruistic Behavior, UCI-Led Study Finds," University of California, Irvine, May 19, 2015, https://news.uci.edu/2015/05/19/awe-promotes-altruistic-behavior-uci-led-study-finds/.

3. Activity adapted from https://t2informatik.de/en/smartpedia/esvp/

4. Victoria Kingdon, "Remove these Two Phrases from Your Vocabulary to be More Successful," *Bazaar*, November 5, 2017, https://www.harpersbazaar.com/uk/guide/a13303288/remove-these -two-phrases-from-your-vocabulary-to-be-more-successful/.
5. Celeste Kidd, Benjamin Y. Hayden, "The Psychology and Neuroscience of Curiosity," *Neuron* 88(3), November 4, 2015, https:// www.sciencedirect.com/science/article/pii/S0896627315007679.

CHAPTER 7

1. Kevin McSpadden, "You Now Have a Shorter Attention Span Than a Goldfish," *Time*, May 14, 2015, https://time.com/3858309/attention -spans-goldfish/.
2. GAIAM, "Breathing is Believing: The Importance of Nasal Breathing," GAIAM.Com, Accessed January 8, 2021, https://www .gaiam.com/blogs/discover/breathing-is-believing-the-importance-of -nasal-breathing.

CHAPTER 8

1. Justin Bariso, "5 Tactics Passive Aggressive People Use to Get Under Your Skin," Inc., November 21, 2018, https://www.inc.com/justin -bariso/5-tactics-passive-aggressive-people-use-to-get-under-your -skin-and-how-you-can-fight-back.html.
2. Paul J. Zak, "The Neuroscience of Trust," *Harvard Business Review*, January-February 2017, https://hbr.org/2017/01/the-neuroscience-of -trust.
3. Jessica Stillman, "This is Exactly How you Win and Lose Trust," *Inc.*, December 10, 2015, https://www.inc.com/jessica-stillman/this -is-exactly-how-you-win-and-lose-trust.html.
4. Linda Bloom and Charlie Bloom, "Why Relationships Can Never be 50-50 Propositions," *Psychology Today*, April 28, 2015, https:// www.psychologytoday.com/us/blog/stronger-the-broken-places /201504/why-relationships-can-never-be-50-50-propositions.
5. Tony Alessandra, "The Official Site of Dr. Tony Alessandra," *Tony Alessandra*, Accessed January 1, 2021, https://www.alessandra.com /abouttony/aboutpr.asp.
6. Tony Alessandra, "The Platinum Rule: What it is and Why it Applies to You," *C-Suite Network*, Accessed January 1, 2021, https:// c-suitenetwork.com/news/the-platinum-rule-what-is-it-and-how -does-it-apply-to-you-2/.

CHAPTER 9

1. Riitta Hari and Miiamaaria V. Kujala, "Brain Basis of Human Social Interaction: From Concepts to Brain Imaging,"

American Physiological Society, April 1, 2009, https://journals .physiology.org/doi/full/10.1152/physrev.00041.2007.

2. Richard Fry, "Millennials Are the Largest Generation in the Workforce," *Pew Research Center,* April 11, 2018, https:// www.pewresearch.org/fact-tank/2018/04/11/millennials -largest-generation-us-labor-force/.

3. Caity Weaver, "Typing These Two Letters Will Scare Your Coworkers," New York Times, December 6, 2019, https:// www.nytimes.com/2019/11/21/business/kk.html.

4. Judith E. Glaser, "*Conversational Intelligence: How Great Leaders Build Trust and Get Extraordinary Results,*" Brookline, MA: Bibliomotion Inc, 2016.

5. David Lappako, "Communication is 93% Non-verbal: An Urban Legend Proliferates," *Communication and Theatre Association of Minnesota Journal,* January 2007, https:// cornerstone.lib.mnsu.edu/cgi/viewcontent.cgi?article=1000& context=ctamj.

6. Pat Schneider, "*Writing Alone and with Others,*" Amherst, Massachusetts, Oxford University Press, 2003.

CHAPTER 10

1. California Institute of Technology, "Scientists uncover why you can't decide what to order for lunch: A new Caltech study finds the brain regions responsible for the choice overload effect," *ScienceDaily,* October 1, 2018, www.sciencedaily.com/releases /2018/10/181001171154.htm.

CHAPTER 12

1. https://belonging.berkeley.edu/

INDEX

Page numbers followed by *f* refer to figures.

Jennifer Edwards is a business and leadership advisor working with Fortune 500 companies and boards, equipping them to perform and collaborate optimally when pressure and stress hit. Her clients include top leaders at global companies, including Microsoft and WeWork. She is a partner at Winning Streak Ventures, an early-stage venture capital fund which invests in disruptive technology companies. Jennifer resides in Granite Bay, CA, with her husband Marty, and has three amazing adult daughters, Allison, Taylor, and Lauryn.

Katie McCleary, MFA, is an entrepreneur and storyteller who trains leaders, creatives, and humanitarians to launch big ideas by leveraging their social and cultural capital. She is the founder of 916 Ink, a nonprofit that has transformed over 4,000 vulnerable youth into confident authors. She is the host of "The Drive" podcast on NPR's CapRadio with the American Leadership Forum-MVC. She resides in Fair Oaks, CA, with her partner Nicholas, their children, and a menagerie of feathered and furry creatures.

Together, we help people show up and communicate better when feeling pressure in their relationships at work, home, and in the community. We design and tailor Bridge the Gap experiences for clients, organizations, and boards to enhance their communication and collaboration skills. Learn more at www.howtobridgethegap.com.